Portfolio Theory and Investment Management

Second Edition

Richard Dobbins, Stephen F. Witt
and John Fielding

First published 1983
Second edition 1994

Blackwell Publishers
108 Cowley Road
Oxford OX4 1JF
UK

238 Main Street
Cambridge, Massachusetts 02142
USA

British Library Cataloguing in Publication Data
A CIP catalogue record for this book is available from the British Library.

Library of Congress Cataloging-in-Publication Data
Dobbins, Richard.
   Portfolio theory and investment management/Richard Dobbins, Stephen F. Witt, and John Fielding.—2nd ed.
      p.   cm.
   Includes bibliographical references and indexes.
   ISBN 0–631–19182–8 (alk. paper)
   1. Portfolio management.   2. Investment analysis.   I. Witt, Stephen F.
   II. Fielding, John.   III. Title.
HG4529.5.D62   1994
332.6–dc20
                                                                93–23965
                                                                      CIP

Typeset in 11 on 13pt Times
by TecSet Ltd.
Printed in Great Britain by Page Bros, Norwich
This book is printed on acid-free paper

Contents

Figures

Tables

Preface

This book provides an introduction to modern portfolio theory and investment management. Our target user is found on MBA, post-experience, undergraduate business studies, finance, accounting, and economics programmes in universities and other colleges. It should also find favour with those people who actually manage portfolios, advise clients on investment policy and enact transactions in securities. The book should provide interesting reading for security analysts, stockbrokers, accountants, lawyers and bankers, who are expected to give informed investment advice to their clients, outlining the risks of investment as well as expected returns.

The material has been used extensively in our own universities on short courses for MBA students, third-year undergraduates in business studies and visiting managers on post-experience programmes. We concentrate on the key ideas in modern portfolio theory; many excellent lengthy texts do this, but also provide a vast quantity of additional material relating to kinds of securities, operation of the stock market, sources of investment information, analysis of financial statements, economic indicators, and detailed expositions of fundamental analysis and chartism. Our brief text does not dwell on this general or background information, but rather on the theoretical ideas developed in recent years in the subject area entitled 'modern portfolio theory' (MPT), and we discuss the implications of MPT for investment management. The book is specifically designed for those students coming to the subject for the first time.

Richard Dobbins
Stephen F. Witt
John Fielding
January 1993

1

The revolution in portfolio theory: a summary

Introduction

Portfolio theory has undergone a revolution in the last 40 years. The fundamental ideas are introduced in this, our first, chapter, which includes discussion of the inevitable trade-off between risk and return, illustrated by the capital asset pricing model. Return and risk are defined and illustrated, and total risk is shown to be made up of market risk and specific risk. Market risk is unavoidable because it arises from movements in the economy as a whole; the specific risk relating to individual companies can be removed by diversification, and efficient capital markets will therefore offer no rewards for specific risk. Diversification thus makes sense for investors, because they can avoid specific risk. We introduce the market model, the security market line, and the Markowitz approach to diversification. The important new ideas in modern portfolio theory are followed by a brief discussion of indexation and active–passive management. Finally, having introduced the important new ideas, we provide a brief note on the traditional approach to portfolio management.

The capital asset pricing model

Modern portfolio theory teaches that there is a trade-off between risk and return. For many years, investment advisers and investment managers focused on returns with the occasional caveat 'subject to risk'. As risk was not understood, not a great deal could be said. Modern portfolio theory (MPT) concentrates on risk at least as much as return. In fact, MPT could be described as risk management, rather than return management. We can make decisions about the risks we are prepared to take but we cannot make decisions about the returns we shall achieve, as these are decided by factors beyond our control, although we would anticipate that the higher the risk, the higher should be the expected return. For example, borrowing money from the bank in order to invest in equities which promise an expected return considerably higher than the bank rate of interest may result in considerable gain, but there is a high risk of substantial loss if equity prices fall. On the other hand, if you place your initial investment in a clearing bank deposit account, the risk of loss is just about zero, but you do expect the return to be the given (low) rate of interest. We would expect other investments, such as unit trusts and quoted ordinary shares, to offer higher returns than bank deposits or government securities because the returns they offer are more volatile – that is, risky. In a rational world we should expect a clear trade-off between risk and return, and the most widely acclaimed description of this trade-off is the capital asset pricing model (CAPM), which is depicted in figure 1.1 by the security market line (SML).

Portfolio (or security) expected returns are measured along the vertical axis, and portfolio (or security) risk is measured along the horizontal axis. As will be discussed later in this chapter, portfolio returns include dividends and capital appreciation. The most widely used measure of portfolio risk is beta (β), which is a measure of the market sensitivity of returns. It represents the extent to which the return of an individual security or portfolio moves with some broad-based market index representative of the total economy. For the time being, figure 1.1 shows that there is a trade-off between risk and return and that the trade-off is positive and linear, each incremental increase in risk being associated with an increase in expected return.

Some investments are virtually zero risk. For example, the return of three-month Treasury bills can be considered as riskless, the probability of default by the government being zero. The return of such risk-free investments is represented by R_F. They offer a small positive return for zero risk. For those who prefer to play for higher returns and accept the associated higher risk, there is the market for quoted ordinary shares (equities, common stocks). The

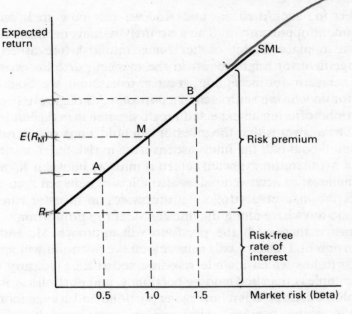

Figure 1.1 Security market line

portfolio M represents the total economy; it is a weighted average of all quoted equities and is generally referred to as the market portfolio. If we invest in this portfolio we expect to earn the return on the market, R_M. This theoretical portfolio is important in the theory of portfolio management because it is a perfectly diversified portfolio. It is almost certain that nobody ever holds this particular portfolio, but a widely diversified equity portfolio could approximate to the market portfolio. Let us assume for the time being that this is the only equity portfolio in which investors are interested. It is more risky than the risk-free investment because returns in the stock market are far more volatile than returns of three-month Treasury bills. We all know that it is possible to make and lose a great deal of money playing the stock market, and even a casual glance at historic share price movements leads us to conclude that prices are highly volatile. The trade-off between risk and return implies that rational investors expect a higher return for investing in the market portfolio than in risk-free assets; they will not always get the higher return, but they must always expect it, otherwise rational investors would switch from equities into Treasury bills.

Having identified R_F and R_M, we can now seek out some investment opportunities. The extremely risk-averse investor might choose to place all his or her funds into risk-free assets, while another investor might invest in the market portfolio expecting a higher return for accepting greater risk. Now what should an investor do who wishes to achieve portfolio A in figure 1.1 – that is, a portfolio offering an expected return greater than R_F but less than R_M? The answer is that the investor can hold a mix of Treasury bills and equities. If half the funds are invested in risk-free securities and half in M, then the expected return is midway between R_F and R_M, and the level of accepted risk is also midway between zero and the risk of the market portfolio. Furthermore, an investor can hold a portfolio anywhere along the line R_F M. If the proportion of equity holdings is increased, the portfolio will approach M, and if the proportion of Treasury bills is increased the portfolio will approach R_F. Portfolios which include risk-free securities (Treasury bills in our example) are called lending portfolios, and portfolio A is such a portfolio. Portfolio B is a borrowing portfolio and is even more risky than the market portfolio. How can we create portfolio B? In our artificial world we have only risk-free securities and M. An investor can place all available resources in M and yet hold portfolio B which has a higher risk and higher expected return than M. Since the expected return of M is higher than the expected return of risk-free assets, the investor can borrow at R_F and invest the funds in M. In a world where borrowing and lending rates are the same (our assumption for the time being), a portfolio can be financed partly by borrowing at R_F, and where this takes place the portfolio is called a borrowing or leveraged portfolio. The investment schedule consists entirely of M, the market portfolio, but the investment schedule is financed partly by borrowing, and the greater the borrowing, the greater the expected return and the greater the market risk. Portfolio M, the market portfolio, represents the UK economy and is subject to market or economic risk. We can increase the risk of the portfolio by leverage. The additional risk arising on the introduction of the leveraged portfolio is the sum of market risk and financial risk. One of the most important ideas in modern portfolio theory is that the expected return of a portfolio is directly related to the riskiness of the portfolio. Furthermore, portfolio risk can be measured by beta.

We shall return to beta very shortly. For the time being, let us end this introductory section with the capital asset pricing model, which states that the expected return of a portfolio is made up of R_F, the risk-free reward for time (delayed consumption), plus a premium for accepting market risk:

$$E(R_p) = R_F + \beta_p[E(R_M) - R_F] \qquad (1.1)$$

where $E(R_p)$ is the expected return of the portfolio, R_F is the risk-free rate of interest, β_p is the portfolio β (market sensitivity index), $E(R_M)$ is the expected return of the market portfolio and $[E(R_M) - R_F]$ is the market risk premium.

If the risk-free rate of interest is 6 per cent and the expected return of the market portfolio is 15 per cent, then the expected return of the portfolio is clearly a linear function of beta. For portfolio betas of (1) 0, (2) 0.5, (3) 1.0, (4) 1.5, and (5) 2, the expected returns are:

1 $E(R_p) = 6 + 0 \,(15 - 6) = 6$ per cent
2 $E(R_p) = 6 + 0.5 \,(15 - 6) = 10.5$ per cent
3 $E(R_p) = 6 + 1.0 \,(15 - 6) = 15$ per cent
4 $E(R_p) = 6 + 1.5 \,(15 - 6) = 19.5$ per cent
5 $E(R_p) = 6 + 2.0 \,(15 - 6) = 24.0$ per cent.

The security market line in figure 1.1 demonstrates the trade-off between market risk and expected return. The capital asset pricing model enables us to estimate the expected return of a portfolio given R_F, R_M and beta.

Return

Positive returns are welcome. This is what investment is all about – delayed consumption and risk-taking in the expectation of greater opportunities for consumption (returns) in the future. We expect rewards for delayed consumption, R_F, and something extra for taking risks, $\beta[E(R_M) - R_F]$. Investors have always been extremely aware of returns, which, as far as investment in equities is concerned, come in two forms – dividends and capital gains. The return of an individual investment or portfolio can be measured as follows:

$$R_t = \frac{P_t - P_{t-1} + D_t}{P_{t-1}} \qquad (1.2)$$

where R_t is the periodic return, P_t is the price at the end of the period, P_{t-1} is the price at the beginning of the period, $P_t - P_{t-1}$ is the capital gain or loss and D_t is the dividend received at the end of the period.

For example, if the value of a portfolio is 100 at the beginning of a period, and 120 at the end of the period after receiving a dividend of 10, then the return of the portfolio is 30 per cent:

$$R_t = \frac{120 - 100 + 10}{100} = 30 \text{ per cent.}$$

The traditional method of investment appraisal concentrated on maximizing returns. A 20 per cent expected return might be considered as acceptable 'subject to risk', although risk was generally not measured. The modern approach focuses on risk.

Risk

Risk is the one-in-six rule. It relates to the volatility of an expected outcome, the dispersion or spread of likely returns around the expected return. In figure 1.2 the expected return of a project is 16 per cent. From statistics, we know that for 68 per cent of the time the actual return will lie within one standard deviation of the expected return. The standard deviation is a measure of dispersion or spread. Approximately four out of six actual outcomes should, on average, lie within one standard deviation of the expected outcome. In figure 1.2, four out of six outcomes should, on average, lie between 10 per cent and 22 per cent, 6 per cent being the standard deviation. This is the good news. The bad news is that two times in

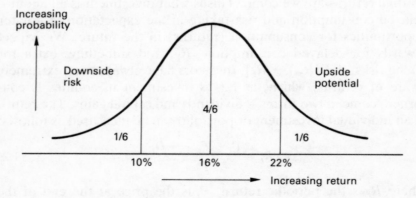

Figure 1.2   Risk is the one-in-six rule

six the outcome can be expected to lie outside one standard deviation. On average, one time in six the outcome will be above 22 per cent, and this is generally referred to as upside potential. Unfortunately, one time in six the actual return is likely to be less than 10 per cent, and this is generally referred to as downside risk. This is the one-in-six rule. Investors do not like risk, and the greater the riskiness of returns of an investment, the greater will be the return expected by investors. There is a trade-off between risk and return which must be reflected in the required rates of return of investment opportunities.

The standard deviation (or variance, which is the standard deviation squared), measures the total risk of an investment. <u>It is not necessary for an investor to accept the total risk of an individual security; investors can and do diversify.</u> Some of the risk associated avoided by with individual investments can be avoided by diversification, and diversifica figure 1.3 shows how some of the total risk associated with individual securities can be avoided by diversification. Investment in Single Sec implies a single security implies acceptance of total risk, so it is not not advise acceptance of total advisable for investors to put all their funds into a single investment for investors risk. as this exposes them to more risk than is necessary for the expected to put in return. Figure 1.3 shows that if we increase the number of invest-single inv.

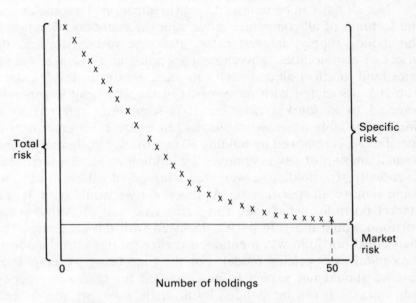

Figure 1.3   Risk reduction by diversification

portfolio risk ↓. ment holdings from 1 to 2, 3, 4 and so on, then we achieve considerable portfolio risk reduction. This happens because the surprise bad news for one company is offset by surprise good news for another company. These good and bad shocks specific to individual companies cancel out each other. Company A launches a successful new product, while Company B launches a failure. Company C has a sudden damaging strike, while Company D makes a breakthrough in design. Company E learns that its products are dangerous to health, while Company F wins a large government contract. These events are specific to individual companies and are unrelated to general movements in the economy. These specific events generally cancel out, and the result of diversification is reduction in portfolio volatility, that is, reduction in portfolio risk. As the number of holdings approaches 50 or 60, a good deal of total *Specific risk* risk is removed by diversification, and this risk which can be removed by diversification is called specific risk, because it is specific to individual companies. Specific risk is sometimes called diversifiable risk, avoidable risk, unique risk or non-market risk, and one of the crucial ideas in modern portfolio theory is that investors should not expect to be rewarded for taking on risk which can be avoided. They should expect to be rewarded only for unavoidable or market risk.

Not all risk can be removed by diversification. To some extent, the fortunes of all companies move with the economy. Changes in the money supply, interest rates, exchange rates, taxation, the prices of commodities, government spending and overseas economies tend to affect all companies to some greater or lesser extent. The risk associated with movements in the economy is generally referred to as market risk, but it is sometimes referred to as non-diversifiable or unavoidable risk. In figure 1.3 a great deal of specific risk is removed by holding 50 securities, but thereafter only a small amount of risk is removed by holding additional securities. Eventually, by holding a weighted average of all securities, we could remove all specific risk. At this point we would hold M, the market portfolio, which has no specific risk, and the value of the portfolio would move in perfect lockstep with the economy. This theoretical portfolio was mentioned earlier, in our introduction to the capital asset pricing model. For the time being we emphasize that we should not expect to be rewarded for taking on specific risk, because it can be avoided by diversification; we should only expect to be rewarded for taking on unavoidable or market risk.

This is a very important idea in modern portfolio theory – the expected return of a security or portfolio should be directly related to the level of market risk associated with that security or portfolio. The capital asset pricing model shows that the expected return of an investment is a positive linear function of market risk (measured by beta).

We must immediately add another important idea in MPT. Market risk can be measured, and the measure is universally referred to as beta. Market risk is non-diversifiable (in fact, UK market risk can be reduced by international diversification, but we ignore this for the time being). Market risk is the risk associated with general movements in the economy and affects all quoted companies to some greater or lesser extent. Unfortunately, there is no readily available measure of general movements in the economy on a day-to-day basis. With a view to measuring the market risk of individual securities and portfolios it is therefore necessary to find a benchmark representing the economy. Such a benchmark in the UK is the broad-based *Financial Times* all-share index. Using this broad-based index as a surrogate for the UK economy, it is possible to measure the extent to which returns of portfolios and individual securities move with unanticipated changes in general economic conditions.

Figure 1.4 shows the change in the periodic returns of three hypothetical securities plotted against the change in the periodic returns of the *Financial Times* (*FT*) all-share index. Let us suppose that the return of a security rises by 10 per cent when the return of the index rises by 10 per cent, and that when the return of the market falls by 10 per cent then the return of the individual security also falls by 10 per cent. If these periodic returns are plotted, then the line of best fit through all the points will be a 45° line as shown for security B. The slope of the line as measured by beta will be 1. The beta coefficient is therefore the measure of a security's market risk. It is a market sensitivity index indicating the extent to which periodic returns of an individual security move with periodic returns of the market.

A high-risk investment, such as security C, might have a beta of 2 (security C might be an investment in a hire-purchase or property company). Its periodic return rises by 20 per cent or falls by 20 per cent when the return of the all-share index rises or falls, respectively, by only 10 per cent. Security A is an example of an investment in a low-risk company, it might be a tea or snuff company, and its

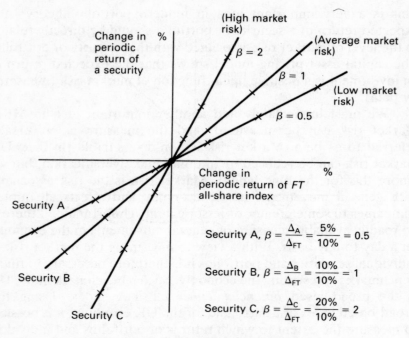

Figure 1.4 Measuring security betas

periodic return rises or falls by 5 per cent when the market return rises or falls, respectively, by 10 per cent. It has a beta of 0.5.

Beta is therefore a market sensitivity index. It measures the extent to which, on average, the periodic return of a security or portfolio moves with the market. Betas are important in MPT because the theory suggests that expected returns are directly related to the level of accepted market risk as measured by beta. The beta of a portfolio is the weighted average of the betas of individual securities making up the portfolio. Furthermore, these betas are now available from several UK sources including the *Risk Measurement Service* publication of the London Business School.

In figure 1.4 all co-ordinates lie on straight lines which pass through the origin. Periodic returns of individual securities A, B and C, move directly with changes in the market return, but we would not expect this to occur in the real world. Securities offer specific returns as well as market returns, so that we should not expect the points to fall exactly on a straight line.

In figure 1.5 the periodic returns of an individual security R_i are plotted against the periodic returns of the *FT* all-share index, R_M.

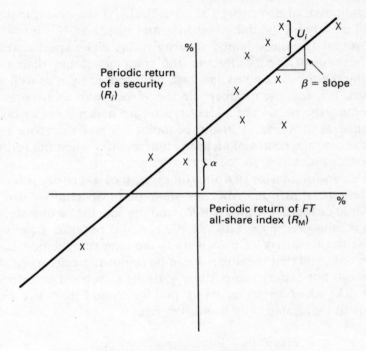

Figure 1.5 Characteristic line

The co-ordinates do not lie exactly on the line of best fit because, as already indicated, companies earn not only returns associated with general movements in the economy but also specific returns associated with corporate decisions and events affecting only the individual company or its industry. The characteristic line, as illustrated in figure 1.5, suggests that there is a linear relationship between the periodic return of an individual security R_i and periodic returns of the market, R_M, and also that the return of the security does not move exactly with the market return. Using least-squares regression analysis, a line of best fit is plotted through the co-ordinates. The relationship between R_i and R_M is given by the market model:

$$R_i = \alpha_i + \beta_i R_M + U_i \qquad (1.3)$$

where R_i is the return of an individual security, α_i is the value of the intercept, β_i is the slope of the characteristic line and U_i is a random error term.

Beta indicates the average sensitivity of returns of an individual security to the market return, and is a measure of the market or systematic risk of a security (or portfolio). As the co-ordinates do not fall exactly on the line of best fit, an error term U is introduced to represent the unexplained security return. The specific returns arise because of events affecting the company rather than events affecting the total economy, and are represented by α as well as U. In figure 1.5, α is the intercept on the vertical axis and represents, on average, the portion of a security's return which is not associated with general movements in the economy. Alpha therefore represents the average return of an individual security when the return of the market index is zero.

We can summarize that the total return of a security is the sum of systematic return and the unsystematic or specific return. The systematic or market return is $\beta_i R_M$ and the specific or unsystematic return is measured by α_i plus U_i. We can also reiterate from figure 1.3 that the total risk of a security is the sum of specific risk and market risk, and that specific risk can be removed by diversification. We should not expect competitive markets to reward investors for taking risks which they can avoid, and we should therefore expect rewards to be related only to market risk.

Diversification

Spreading the risk, or diversification, makes good sense for investors. It removes specific, unique, diversifiable, non-market risk, but diversification does not remove market risk (other than by international diversification). The purchaser of a share in a quoted company gets two investments for the price of one – an investment in the UK economy and an investment in the company earning returns specific to the individual company. One of the attractive features of MPT is that it explains the way in which shareholders have always behaved; they have always held diversified portfolios. Modern portfolio theory suggests that diversification is rational, given that investors should only take on that part of risk for which they expect to be rewarded.

The pioneering work in modern portfolio theory, and risk quantification in particular, is attributable to Harry Markowitz (1952). Some 40 years ago he suggested that, for any given level of risk, the rational investor would select the maximum expected return, and that for any given level of expected return, the rational investor would select the minimum risk. Before Markowitz, investment analysts talked about maximizing returns – subject to risk.

Harry Markowitz laid down the cornerstones of modern portfolio theory by measuring risk.

Let us suppose that the stock market is made up of 100 quoted equities. With a view to developing a series of possible portfolios, it would be necessary to estimate the expected return of each security. The expected return of any portfolio or mix of equities would be a weighted average of the expected returns of each security in the portfolio. Risk is more complicated because it is not a weighted average. First, it would be necessary to estimate the variance (or standard deviation) of the expected return for each security. This is a measure of volatility or risk. For 100 equities we would be faced with the difficult task of estimating 100 variances or standard deviations. Secondly, it would be necessary to estimate how returns of every individual security would move or covary with those of every other individual security. This is obviously an extremely difficult task, but we would expect returns of securities in the same industry to move in the same direction, while returns of investments in different industries would not move in lockstep. In fact, we would clearly expect to reduce total risk or variance by diversification. As already discussed, we would not expect to remove risk completely, but we would expect to remove or significantly reduce specific, unique or non-market risk.

In figure 1.6 the shaded area represents the set of portfolios which can be generated with the available equities. Each portfolio is

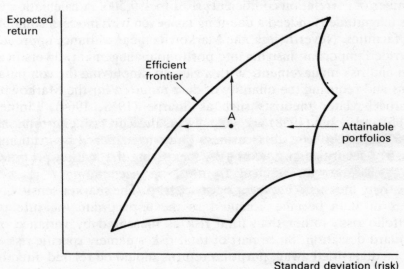

Figure 1.6   Markowitz mean-variance approach

attainable, though not necessarily desirable. For example, portfolio A is an attainable but inefficient portfolio. It is possible to accept the total risk associated with portfolio A and move vertically upwards to find a portfolio on the efficient frontier offering a higher expected return for the same risk. Alternatively, for the expected return associated with portfolio A, it is possible to move horizontally to the left and find a portfolio on the efficient frontier offering the same expected return for lower risk. One of the maxims of the Markowitz approach is that the rational investor prefers the maximum expected return for any level of risk, and the minimum risk for any level of expected return. The efficient frontier in figure 1.6 identifies those portfolios offering the maximum expected return for any level of risk and those portfolios offering the minimum risk for any level of expected return. Having identified the efficient set of portfolios, the investor can select that portfolio on the efficient frontier which satisfies his or her risk–return preference.

The main problem in applying the Markowitz approach to portfolio management is the large amount of data which is required. For example, for a portfolio of 100 securities we need 100 expected returns and 100 variances. In addition, we need the number of correlation coefficients between each of the securities in the portfolio. This is given by the formula $n(n - 1)/2$ where n is the number of securities. Thus, for this example, $100(100 - 1)/2$ or 4,950 correlation coefficients are required. For a portfolio of 1,000 securities the number of correlation coefficients rises to 499,500. A calculation of this magnitude is indeed a daunting task even with modern computing facilities. Nevertheless, the Markowitz mean-variance approach provided important insights into portfolio management, diversification and risk management. With a view to simplifying the computations and reducing the quantity of data required for the Markowitz approach, later theorists such as Sharpe (1963, 1964), Lintner (1965) and Tobin (1958) side-stepped the difficult task of estimating covariances between all securities. This was achieved by including risk-free securities in the analysis, identifying the market portfolio on the Markowitz efficient frontier, and generating a market sensitivity measure (beta) for each security. The market sensitivity index or beta became accepted as the appropriate measure of portfolio risk, rather than total risk as measured by variance or standard deviation. Since part of total risk – namely specific risk – can be diversified away, portfolio returns should be related directly to unavoidable or market risk. In short, the computational difficulties of correlating the returns of all securities with each other were overcome by measuring the sensitivity of return of each security to the market return.

The reader should recognize that we are again discussing the capital asset pricing model. The Markowitz approach, as illustrated in figure 1.6, deals with all-equity portfolios. Once we introduce the risk-free rate of interest, we can generate the capital market line as illustrated in figure 1.7, from which it is possible to derive the security market line. The Markowitz efficient frontier of all-equity portfolios is shown in figure 1.7. We now add R_F, the zero-risk small positive return of three-month Treasury bills, and draw a line which just touches the Markowitz efficient frontier at M, the market portfolio. The only portfolio which has no specific risk at all is M, the weighted average of all equities. This is the only efficient all-equity portfolio once we introduce risk-free assets. Investors may hold the market at M or invest some of their funds in risk-free assets. For those investors who seek an even higher risk than the market level, it is possible to add financial risk to economic risk by borrowing and investing in M. As the market portfolio has no specific risk, all portfolios along the capital market line (CML) are theoretically efficient in that they have no specific risk, and the expected return of any portfolio along the CML is a function of the

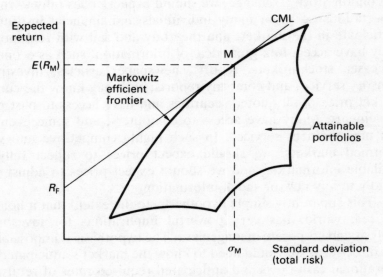

Figure 1.7   Capital market line

total risk of the portfolio. The security market line (SML), which relates expected return to beta for individual securities and portfolios, may be derived from the CML. We can now use the capital asset pricing model (1.1), as illustrated in figure 1.1, to estimate the return of any portfolio, as follows:

$$E(R_p) = R_F + \beta_p[E(R_M) - R_F].$$

The expected return of a portfolio is equal to the risk-free rate of interest plus a premium for market risk. The higher the beta, the greater the risk premium. If R_F is 6 per cent and $E(R_M)$ is 15 per cent, then the risk premium for the market is 9 per cent. A portfolio with a beta of 0.5 has an average expected return of 10.5 per cent and a portfolio with a beta of 2 has an average expected return of 24 per cent.

The efficient market hypothesis

One of the most important ideas in modern portfolio theory is the efficient market hypothesis (EMH). The EMH suggests that share prices fully reflect all available information, any new or shock information being immediately incorporated into the share price. In highly competitive markets, such as the New York Stock Exchange or London Stock Exchange, we should expect prices fully to reflect expectations. A great many individuals and financial institutions participate in the market, and they buy and sell with real money. They have access to a great deal of information, such as economic forecasts, stockbrokers' reports, newspaper articles, investment advisory services and company reports, and they know the current market price of all quoted securities and have access to past price movements. Many have access to computers, and some even use risk measurement services. In such highly competitive and well-informed markets, we should expect prices to reflect fully all available information, and we should expect prices to adjust very rapidly to any new or shock information.

This apparently simple hypothesis, to the extent that it holds in the real world, has very powerful implications for investment analysis and corporate management. The hypothesis is impossible to test directly, as we would need to know the market's anticipated net operational cash flows and anticipated required rates of return for all future periods, and also all information relevant to security prices and the way this information is reflected in prices. It is therefore necessary to design tests of the hypothesis based on available information and available statistical techniques. Tests of the EMH are generally made under the assumptions of zero transaction costs, no taxation, free access to all available information for all traders, and agreement among them as to the implications of information for security prices. A great deal of evidence supports the hypothesis, such evidence appearing in three forms – the weak form, the semi-strong form and the strong form. Weak form tests of the EMH are concerned with the extent to which share prices can be used to predict future prices, and a great deal of evidence suggests that the historic series of prices cannot predict future prices. Semi-strong form tests attempt to measure the extent to which share prices fully reflect all publicly available information. Investors anticipate and react to publicly available information relating to stock splits, earnings announcements, dividend announcements, forecasts and large block trades. Most of the research suggests that it is extremely difficult to earn excess returns using publicly available information. Finally, strong form tests are designed to discover whether share prices reflect all information, even information which is not available to the public. The studies are generally concerned with the stock market performance of professional investors and fund managers, and most of the evidence suggests that the professionals do not have access to techniques enabling them to earn returns greater than returns expected for the level of expected market risk.

Some evidence against the EMH is available. Stock market specialists and corporate insiders have monopolistic access to information, which, on occasions, enables them to earn superior returns. Furthermore, there is some evidence that some people do have better forecasting ability than the rest of us. It is therefore possible to beat the EMH – but it is extremely difficult. Modern stock markets do appear to be efficient, in that share prices do reflect all available information, any new information being very rapidly incorporated into the share price in an unbiased way by the competitive trading activities of many investors. However, there is some evidence which suggests that the stock market exhibits greater volatility than could be attributed to any rational analysis of fundamental factors. This will be discussed in more detail in chapter 6.

The efficient market hypothesis is extremely bad news for those course participants who came along to learn how to make easy money. The EMH generally comes as a rather disappointing but readily acceptable surprise to MBA students, third-year undergraduates, and corporate managers. Surely, the competitive activities of a great many traders should generate the equilibrium price where security prices reflect all available information. It is not until we introduce the implications of the EMH that our audience becomes alarmed, even hostile. In efficient markets, investors pay the market price for acquisitions. There are no bargains. Share price movements cannot be predicted from past price movments – even with computerized forecasting models. Company earnings and dividend announcements are generally anticipated and should not result in wild share price movements. Only the shocks cause movements in security prices. There are no mechanical systems for making money.

Naturally, the efficient market hypothesis is very unpopular, particularly with stock market professionals and investment advisers, since their incomes depend on persuading investors that they can make money through profitable trading. The bad news is that a vast quantity of research supports the hypothesis. The good news is that the investor can beat the EMH with luck, inside information, or forecasting ability. As for the rest of us, we should only expect to be rewarded for the amount of market risk we accept.

Modern investment management

Modern investment management is based on risk management. Various risk measurement services offer the necessary data. If an investor accepts the efficient market hypothesis and the capital asset pricing model, then there is no point in trying to achieve returns in excess of those offered for accepting market risk as measured by beta. The investor must decide on the level of market risk he or she is prepared to accept, bearing in mind that, on average, rewards are related to market risk. Diversification removes specific risk, so the market portfolio, or a reasonable approximation, should be held by all investors. Risk can be reduced or increased by the use of leverage. Investors do not have to build their own portfolios, since indexation services offer a vehicle to investors whereby performance is linked to some index.

Investors do not have to accept the EMH or the CAPM, as they can take the Markowitz approach to investment management. Furthermore, they can still make use of modern risk measurement services. An investor who chooses to forecast market movements will hold a high-beta portfolio in an anticipated bull market, and a zero-beta portfolio in an anticipated bear market. The investor who chooses to speculate in some small sector of the market will seek out those securities which usually show extreme volatility – that is, those securities with high specific returns. With forecasting ability, the forecaster will invest in individual companies promising high positive excess returns, and possibly even sell short when predicting negative excess returns.

Most investors will not know whether or not they have forecasting ability, and for them, active–passive management offers the inevitable compromise. They can accept the EMH and CAPM for 90 per cent of the portfolio, which can be passively managed or indexed, and the investor or portfolio manager can try his or her luck or forecasting ability with the remaining 10 per cent. The performance of this actively managed section of the portfolio can be measured over many periods in the search for excess returns. The costs of active management can be justified by excess returns. It can be very difficult to establish forecasting ability, but over the 30-year working life of an investment manager, consistently positive excess returns make a significant difference to the final value of the pension fund. For the student and practitioner, the revolution in portfolio theory offers scope for mental gymnastics as well as a systematic approach to investment management.

The traditional approach to investment management: a note

The traditional approach to portfolio management concerns itself with the investor, definition of portfolio objectives, investment strategy, diversification and selection of individual investments as detailed below:

1 Study the investor:
   (a) Age, health, responsibilities, other assets, portfolio needs.
   (b) Need for income, capital maintenance, liquidity.
   (c) Attitude towards risk.
   (d) Taxation status.

2 Define portfolio objectives:
   (a) To maximize the investor's wealth – subject to risk.

3 Investment strategy:
   (a) Balance fixed-interest securities against equities.

(b) Balance high-dividend-payout companies against high-earnings-growth companies as required.

(c) Find the income or growth portfolio as required.

(d) Balance income tax payable against capital gains tax.

(e) Balance transaction costs against capital gains from rapid switching.

(f) Retain some liquidity to seize upon bargains.

4 Diversification:

(a) Diversification reduces the volatility of returns; that is, diversification reduces risk.

(b) Ten per cent of the equity portfolio in ten different industries provides adequate equity diversification.

(c) Balance equities against fixed-interest securities.

5 Select individual investments:

(a) Devise methods for selecting successful investments by calculating the true or intrinsic value of a share and comparing that value with the current market value (fundamental analysis). Alternatively, try to predict future share prices from past price movements (technical analysis).

(b) Get expert advice, for example from a bank manager, stockbroker or accountant.

(c) Study published accounts closely and try to predict the intrinsic value.

(d) Seek out widely diversified growth companies.

(e) Switch quickly from losers to winners.

(f) Try to obtain inside information to beat the market.

(g) Follow newspaper tipsters with a good track record.

(h) Locate those companies with the right packaging – that is, appropriate dividend and leverage policies.

(i) Locate companies with good asset backing, dividend growth, good earnings records, high quality of management.

The reader of this book should be well equipped to return to these notions later and find many of them to be contradictory, irrational, costly and misleading.

Further reading

Cohen, J. B., E. D. Zinbarg and A. Zeikel: *Investment Analysis and Portfolio Management*, 5th edn, Homewood, Ill., Richard Irwin, 1987.

Elton, E. J., and M. J. Gruber: *Modern Portfolio Theory and Investment Analysis*, 4th edn, New York, John Wiley, 1991.
Lorie, J. H., P. Dodd and M. H. Kimpton: *The Stock Market: Theories and Evidence*, 2nd edn, Homewood, Ill., Richard Irwin, 1985.

2

The mean-variance approach
to portfolio management

Uncertainty and utility theory

Portfolio theory is concerned with the allocation of an individual's wealth among the various available assets. The initial stage in constructing a portfolio is to specify the objective to be pursued, and this may be stated in terms of the individual's utility function. The theoretical foundations of utility theory are therefore examined in the context of the portfolio selection problem. Now as the future value of any given asset is unknown, the problem is one of decision-making under conditions of uncertainty.

The traditional theory of consumer behaviour does not include an analysis of situations involving uncertainty: the individual is only permitted to make choices among riskless alternatives. A risky situation implies that the outcomes of the alternative choices available to the investor are known only in probabilistic form, and modern utility theory (which stems from the work of von Neumann and Morgenstern (1947)) has been developed specifically to accommodate such conditions. Whereas in traditional theory the individual maximizes utility, the corresponding criterion in the modern theory is that a rational individual operating under uncertainty maximizes expected utility. In order to ensure 'rational' behaviour, it is assumed that certain crucial axioms are satisfied, and these are listed in the appendix to this chapter. The calculation of expected utility may then be used to determine the consumer's choices in situations involving risk.

In general, individuals experience diminishing marginal utility of wealth; that is, successively smaller increments of utility are derived from each additional unit of wealth accumulated. This implies that individuals are risk-averse, and in order to accommodate this notion it is usually assumed that individuals possess quadratic utility functions. In general, this appears to be a reasonable approximation. Hence

$$U(W) = \alpha + \beta W - \gamma W^2 \qquad (2.1)$$

where U denotes utility, W denotes wealth, and α, β and γ are arbitrary constants which vary from individual to individual, with $\beta > 0$ and $\gamma > 0$. Now as the individual wishes to maximize expected utility, the expectations operator E must be applied to equation (2.1), which yields

$$E[U(W)] = \alpha + \beta E(W) - \gamma E(W^2). \qquad (2.2)$$

However, since

$$V(W) = E(W^2) - [E(W)]^2 \qquad (2.3)$$

where V denotes variance, equation (2.2) may be rewritten as

$$E[U(W)] = \alpha + \beta E(W) - \gamma [E(W)]^2 - \gamma V(W). \qquad (2.4)$$

Hence, the use of quadratic utility functions permits the specification of the expected utility of an action (which may have a large number of possible outcomes, each with an associated probability of occurrence) merely in terms of the mean and variance of the outcome, as well as implying risk-averting behaviour.

Investment decisions are generally based on the concept of rate of return rather than terminal wealth. It can be shown, however, that at a given level of initial wealth, for every quadratic utility function specified in terms of wealth, a corresponding quadratic utility function may be derived specified in terms of rate of return (see, for example, Ryan (1978), pp. 19–20). Thus equation (2.4) may be restated as

$$E[U(W)] = a + bE(R) - c[E(R)]^2 - cV(R) \qquad (2.5)$$

where R denotes rate of return. and a, b and c are arbitrary constants which vary among individuals, with $b > 0$ and $c > 0$. Now an indifference curve is the locus of points along which expected utility is constant, and it can be seen from equation (2.5) that this may be achieved by different combinations of $E(R)$ and $V(R)$. Indifference curves are thus defined in terms of a trade-off between expected rate of return and variance of the rate of return.

The Markowitz mean-variance formulation

Selection of the optimal portfolio

Modern portfolio theory is concerned with the choice of efficient combinations of assets, and its foundation lies in the work of Markowitz (1952, 1959). Although investors have long been aware, in a qualitative sense, of the benefits resulting from diversification of security holdings, the Markowitz model represented the first substantial quantitative analysis of these benefits. The assumptions underlying the model are as follows:

1 The return on an investment adequately summarizes the outcome of the investment, and investors visualize a probability distribution of rates of return.
2 Investors' risk estimates are proportional to the variance of return they perceive for a security or portfolio.
3 Investors are willing to base their decisions on just two parameters of the probability distribution function – the expected return and variance of return.
4 The investor exhibits risk aversion, so for a given expected return he prefers minimum risk. Obviously, for a given level of risk the investor prefers maximum expected return.

In general, diversification of asset holdings permits a reduction in the variance of return, even for the same level of expected return.

The expected return of a portfolio comprising n securities is the weighted average of the expected return of each security in the portfolio:

$$E(R) = \sum_{i=1}^{n} X_i \mu_i \qquad (2.6)$$

where $E(R)$ is the expected return of the portfolio, X_i is the proportion of security i in the portfolio and μ_i is the expected return of security i. The simplest case is the two-asset portfolio, and here equation (2.6) reduces to

$$E(R) = X_1 \mu_1 + (1 - X_1)\mu_2. \qquad (2.7)$$

Now the risk of a portfolio is measured by the variance of its return, and this is determined by the variance of return of each security and also by the covariance of returns between each pair of securities:

$$V(R) = \sum_{i=1}^{n} X_i^2 \sigma_i^2 + 2 \sum_{i=1}^{n-1} \sum_{j=i+1}^{n} X_i X_j \sigma_{ij} \tag{2.8}$$

where $V(R)$ is the variance of return of the portfolio, σ_i^2 is the variance of return of security i, and σ_{ij} is the covariance of returns between securities i and j. The latter component measures the extent to which the returns move together, and it depends on the correlation of returns between the two securities and the variances of their returns:

$$\sigma_{ij} = \rho_{ij} \sigma_i \sigma_j \tag{2.9}$$

where ρ_{ij} is the correlation coefficient between the returns of securities i and j. Substituting equation (2.9) into equation (2.8) gives

$$V(R) = \sum_{i=1}^{n} X_i^2 \sigma_i^2 + 2 \sum_{i=1}^{n-1} \sum_{j=i+1}^{n} X_i X_j \rho_{ij} \sigma_i \sigma_j. \tag{2.10}$$

It is important to note that the variance of return of a portfolio is determined by the correlation of returns between each pair of securities, as well as the variance of return of each security. In the two-asset portfolio situation, equation (2.10) reduces to

$$V(R) = X_1^2 \sigma_1^2 + (1 - X_1)^2 \sigma_2^2 + 2X_1(1 - X_1)\rho_{12}\sigma_1\sigma_2. \tag{2.11}$$

In order to ascertain the effect of the correlation of returns between securities on the variance of return of a portfolio, equation (2.11) may be examined more closely. It is supposed for simplicity that $\sigma_1 = \sigma_2 = \sigma$. If all investment takes place in security 1, then

$$V(R) = 1.\sigma_1^2 = \sigma^2. \tag{2.12}$$

Similarly if all investment takes place in security 2, then

$$V(R) = 1.\sigma_2^2 = \sigma^2. \tag{2.13}$$

If some investment occurs in both securities, however (that is, diversification takes place), then

$$V(R) = X_1^2 \sigma^2 + (1 - X_1)^2 \sigma^2 + 2X_1(1 - X_1)\rho_{12}\sigma^2$$
$$= \sigma^2[X_1^2 + (1 - X_1)^2 + 2X_1(1 - X_1)\rho_{12}]. \tag{2.14}$$

But it can be seen that

$$[X_1 + (1 - X_1)]^2 = 1 = X_1^2 + (1 - X_1)^2 + 2X_1(1 - X_1).$$
$$(2.15)$$

Substituting equation (2.15) into equation (2.14) shows that

$$V(R) = \sigma^2 \qquad (2.16)$$

if $\rho_{12} = 1$. If $\rho_{12} < 1$, however, then

$$V(R) = \sigma^2 \text{ (a number} < 1) < \sigma^2. \qquad (2.17)$$

Therefore there are always gains from diversification in terms of reducing the variance of return for a given level of expected returns, provided that the returns of the two securities included in the portfolio are not perfectly positively correlated. Low correlation of returns between the securities results in low variance of return of the portfolio, and, in particular, negatively correlated returns result in substantial risk reduction benefits. It is clear that risk can only be eliminated totally if the third term on the right-hand side of equation (2.11) is negative and equal in absolute magnitude to the sum of the first two terms (since the latter are always positive). In practice, however, returns on securities tend to be highly positively correlated, as they are all influenced by the same economic and political factors. Hence, only a certain part of total risk may be eliminated by diversification, and this is known as diversifiable or unsystematic risk. Diversification therefore permits the specific risk relating to individual securities to be removed, but not the systematic (or market) risk. It has been shown empirically by Newbould and Poon (1993) that investment in 50 to 60 randomly selected securities removes a high proportion of diversifiable risk.

In order to determine the proportions in which securities 1 and 2 should be combined in order to minimize the portfolio risk, equation (2.11) may be partially differentiated with respect to X_1 and the result set equal to zero:

$$\begin{aligned}
\frac{\partial V(R)}{\partial X_1} &= 2X_1\sigma_1^2 - 2(1 - X_1)\sigma_2^2 \\
&\quad + [2(1 - X_1) - 2X_1]\rho_{12}\sigma_1\sigma_2 \\
&= X_1(2\sigma_1^2 + 2\sigma_2^2 - 4\rho_{12}\sigma_1\sigma_2) \\
&\quad - 2\sigma_2^2 + 2\rho_{12}\sigma_1\sigma_2.
\end{aligned} \qquad (2.18)$$

For minimum $V(R)$, $\partial V(R)/\partial X_1 = 0$. Hence the risk-minimizing value of X_1 is given by

$$X_1 = \frac{\sigma_2^2 - \rho_{12}\sigma_1\sigma_2}{\sigma_1^2 + \sigma_2^2 - 2\rho_{12}\sigma_1\sigma_2} \cdot \qquad (2.19)$$

The minimum portfolio risk that is possible with this pair of securities may therefore be calculated, along with the portfolio expected rate of return at this minimum risk level.

The Markowitz formulation does not determine a single optimal portfolio. It provides a series of portfolios which are efficient in terms of risk and return in that each portfolio offers the maximum expected return corresponding to a given level of risk, or the minimum risk corresponding to a given level of expected return. The problem can be formulated as the minimization of an objective function subject to constraints. The objective function f incorporates the concept of trading off risk against return and is given by:

$$f = -A[E(R)] + V(R), \quad 0 \leqslant A \leqslant \infty \qquad (2.20)$$

where A is a risk aversion index. If $A = 0$, the portfolio with the lowest variance of return will be selected. As A increases, the investor becomes more willing to accept risk in order to achieve a higher expected return, and if $A = \infty$ the portfolio with the highest expected return will be optimal. The first constraint is that negative investment (selling short) is not permitted:

$$X_i \geqslant 0 \qquad (2.21)$$

and the second is that the portfolio consists of n securities:

$$\sum_{i=1}^{n} X_i = 1. \qquad (2.22)$$

The minimization of equation (2.20) subject to constraints (2.21) and (2.22) may be carried out using the technique of quadratic programming, since the objective function is non-linear while the constraints are linear. A set of efficient portfolios results, each portfolio corresponding to a particular value of the risk aversion index. The solution is represented graphically in figure 2.1. (In fact, more recently, the concept of standard deviation of return has replaced variance of return as the generally accepted measure of risk – see, for example, Brealey and Myers (1991), Copeland and Weston (1988) and Francis (1991). The standard deviation is the square root of the variance – the arguments are unaffected by whichever risk measure is used.)

The shaded area represents all attainable portfolios – that is, all the combinations of risk and expected return which may be

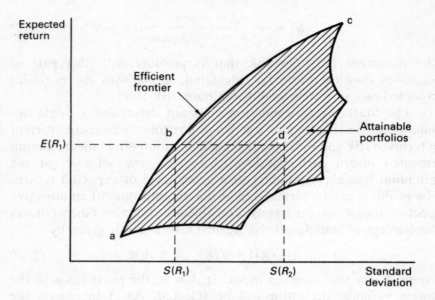

Figure 2.1   Markowitz efficient frontier

achieved with the available securities. The efficient frontier denotes all possible efficient portfolios, and any point on the frontier dominates any point to the right of it. As an illustration, consider the portfolios represented by points b and d. Portfolios b and d promise the same expected return, $E(R_1)$, but the risk associated with b is $S(R_1)$, whereas that associated with d is $S(R_2)$. Investors therefore prefer portfolios on the efficient frontier rather than interior portfolios, given the assumption of risk aversion. Obviously, point a on the frontier represents the portfolio with the least possible risk, while c represents the portfolio with the highest possible rate of return.

The investor has to select a portfolio from among all those represented by the efficient frontier: this will depend upon his risk–return preference. As discussed earlier in this chapter, it is assumed that investors possess quadratic utility functions, and a set of three such indifference curves, U_1, U_2 and U_3, is shown in figure 2.2. The individual is indifferent between any combination of expected return and standard deviation on a particular curve; that is, his utility is constant along the curve. Successively higher indifference curves represent successively higher levels of utility, since, for a given risk level, expected return increases. The investor

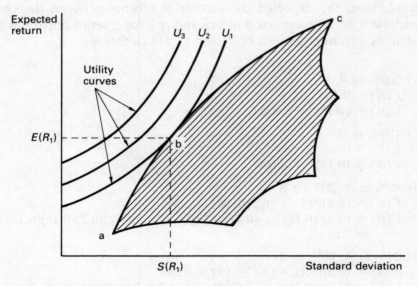

Figure 2.2   Selection of the optimal portfolio

therefore wishes to be on the highest possible indifference curve in order to obtain the maximum possible level of utility, and this is given by the point of tangency between an indifference curve and the efficient frontier – that is, point b. This point therefore represents the optimal portfolio. Different individuals have different utility preferences with respect to expected return and risk (represented by different sets of parameters in equation (2.5)), and therefore the optimal portfolio of securities varies considerably among individuals.

Two-asset example

The securities of companies A and B have the following expected returns and standard deviations of return.

	μ(%)	σ(%)
Company A	10	15
Company B	8	12

In addition, the expected correlation of returns between the two stocks is 0.20. The expected return and risk for a set of portfolios is calculated from equations (2.7) and (2.11) as follows:

(1) 100% in A
$E(R) = 0.10$
$V(R) = (0.15)^2 = 0.0225.$

(2) 100% in B
$E(R) = 0.08$
$V(R) = (0.12)^2 = 0.0144.$

(3) 80% in A, 20% in B
$E(R) = (0.8)(0.1) + (0.2)(0.08) = 0.096$
$V(R) = (0.8)^2(0.15)^2 + (0.2)^2(0.12)^2 + 2(0.8)(0.2)(0.2)(0.15)(0.12)$
   $= 0.0161.$

(4) 20% in A, 80% in B
$E(R) = (0.2)(0.1) + (0.8)(0.08) = 0.084$
$V(R) = (0.2)^2(0.15)^2 + (0.8)^2(0.12)^2 + 2(0.2)(0.8)(0.2)(0.15)(0.12)$
   $= 0.0113.$

(5) 60% in A, 40% in B
$E(R) = (0.6)(0.1) + (0.4)(0.08) = 0.092$
$V(R) = (0.6)^2(0.15)^2 + (0.4)^2(0.12)^2 + 2(0.6)(0.4)(0.2)(0.15)(0.12)$
   $= 0.0121.$

(6) 40% in A, 60% in B
$E(R) = (0.4)(0.1) + (0.6)(0.08) = 0.088$
$V(R) = (0.4)^2(0.15)^2 + (0.6)^2(0.12)^2 + 2(0.4)(0.6)(0.2)(0.15)(0.12)$
   $= 0.0105.$

(7) 50% in A, 50% in B
$E(R) = (0.5)(0.1) + (0.5)(0.08) = 0.09$
$V(R) = (0.5)^2(0.15)^2 + (0.5)^2(0.12)^2 + 2(0.5)(0.5)(0.2)(0.15)(0.12)$
   $= 0.0110.$

If the correlation of returns between the securities is varied, there is no change in portfolio expected return; the effects of different correlations on portfolio risk are summarized in table 2.1. The attainable portfolios derived from table 2.1 are shown in figure 2.3.

If the value $\rho = -1$ is substituted into equation (2.19), then it can be seen that in order to minimize portfolio risk 44 per cent of the portfolio should comprise securities in company A and 56 per cent securities in company B. The portfolio expected return in this case is

Table 2.1   *Two-asset portfolios with varying correlations (example)*

Portfolio	$E(R)$	$S(R) = \sqrt{V(R)}$				
		$\rho = -1$	$\rho = -0.2$	$\rho = 0$	$\rho = 0.2$	$\rho = 1$
(1)	0.100	0.150	0.150	0.150	0.150	0.150
(2)	0.080	0.120	0.120	0.120	0.120	0.120
(3)	0.096	0.096	0.118	0.122	0.128	0.144
(4)	0.084	0.066	0.095	0.100	0.106	0.126
(5)	0.092	0.042	0.093	0.102	0.110	0.138
(6)	0.088	0.012	0.084	0.094	0.103	0.132
(7)	0.090	0.015	0.086	0.096	0.105	0.135

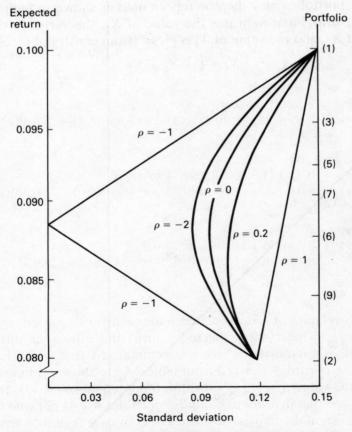

Figure 2.3   *Attainable and efficient portfolios (example)*

0.089, and the portfolio risk is zero. Hence, with perfectly negatively correlated returns, risk can be eliminated.

Examination of figure 2.3 indicates that portfolios (1), (3), (5) and (7) are efficient for correlations of returns between the securities of -1, -0.2, 0, and 0.2. When the returns on the two securities are perfectly positively correlated, however, all the portfolios are efficient.

Geometric analysis of efficient portfolios

Markowitz (1952, 1959) has also provided a geometric representation of his efficient set theory, and this can easily be explained for a three-security universe (which permits a two-dimensional portrayal). Portfolios may then be represented as shown in figure 2.4. The horizontal axis indicates the value of X_1, the vertical axis the value of X_2, and the value of X_3 is given (from constraint (2.22)) by

$$X_3 = 1 - X_1 - X_2. \tag{2.23}$$

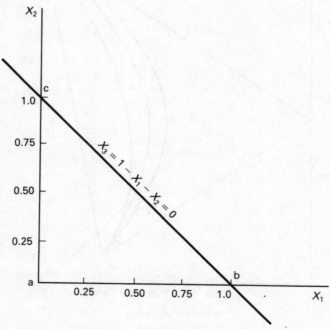

Figure 2.4   Geometric representation of portfolios

Together with constraint (2.21), equation (2.23) implies that the set of attainable portfolios lies in or on the triangle abc, since anywhere outside this area requires negative investment.

In the three-security case, equation (2.6) reduces to

$$E(R) = X_1\mu_1 + X_2\mu_2 + X_3\mu_3. \tag{2.24}$$

If equation (2.23) is substituted into equation (2.24), this yields

$$E(R) = X_1(\mu_1 - \mu_3) + X_2(\mu_2 - \mu_3) + \mu_3. \tag{2.25}$$

Equation (2.25) relates the expected return of the portfolio to the amounts invested in securities 1 and 2. For given values of μ_1, μ_2 and μ_3, the locus of points where $E(R)$ is constant is given by a straight line, known as an iso-mean line. A set of several such iso-mean lines is shown in figure 2.5, where the expected portfolio return increases from left to right.

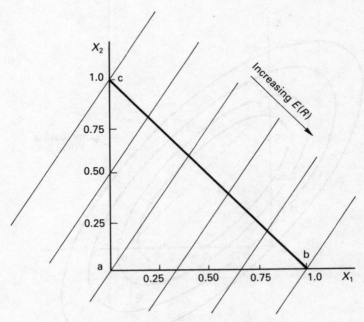

Figure 2.5   Set of iso-mean lines

The variance of return of a portfolio in the three-security case is given (from equation (2.10)) by

$$V(R) = X_1^2\sigma_1^2 + X_2^2\sigma_2^2 + X_3^2\sigma_3^2 + 2X_1X_2\rho_{12}\sigma_1\sigma_2$$
$$+ 2X_1X_3\rho_{13}\sigma_1\sigma_3 + 2X_2X_3\rho_{23}\sigma_2\sigma_3. \tag{2.26}$$

If equation (2.23) is substituted into equation (2.26), then the variance of return of the portfolio is simply expressed as a function of X_1 and X_2:

$$V(R) = X_1^2(\sigma_1^2 - 2\rho_{13}\sigma_1\sigma_3 + \sigma_3^2)$$
$$+ X_2^2(\sigma_2^2 - 2\rho_{23}\sigma_2\sigma_3 + \sigma_3^2)$$
$$+ 2X_1X_2(\rho_{12}\sigma_1\sigma_2 - \rho_{13}\sigma_1\sigma_3 - \rho_{23}\sigma_2\sigma_3 + \sigma_3^2)$$
$$+ 2X_1(\rho_{13}\sigma_1\sigma_3 - \sigma_3^2) + 2X_2(\rho_{23}\sigma_2\sigma_3 - \sigma_3^2)$$
$$+ \sigma_3^2. \tag{2.27}$$

It can be shown that, for given values of σ_1, σ_2, σ_3, ρ_{12}, ρ_{13} and ρ_{23}, the locus of points where $V(R)$ is constant is given by an ellipse, known as an iso-variance curve. A set of several such iso-variance curves is shown in figure 2.6, the variance of return increasing from the centre (point d) outwards.

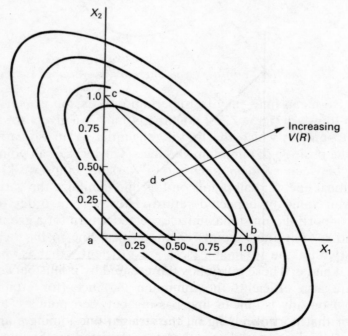

Figure 2.6   Set of iso-variance curves

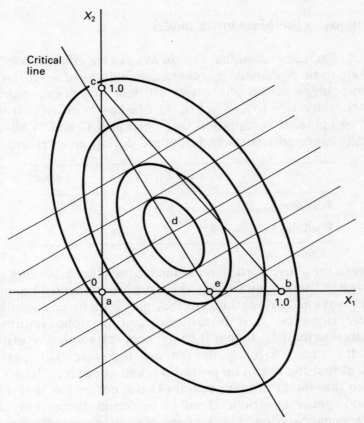

Figure 2.7 Interaction of iso-mean lines and iso-variance curves

The iso-mean lines may be superimposed on the iso-variance curves as shown in figure 2.7. Of all the points on a given iso-mean line, that point at which the line is tangential to an iso-variance curve is the position of minimum variance. The locus of all points of tangency between iso-mean lines and iso-variance ellipses is known as the critical line, and all points on this line minimize the variance for a given value of expected return. However, in order to be efficient, a portfolio must maximize expected return for a given risk level, and so only those points on the critical line to the right of point d (within the attainable set) are efficient – that is, points between d and e. Those portfolios represented by points between e and b are also efficient; the minimum variance (for attainable portfolios) on any iso-mean line passing between points e and b occurs for that portfolio lying on the straight line joining e and b. The set of efficient portfolios is therefore depicted by the line deb.

Objections to the Markowitz model

Baumol (1963) has noted that certain Markowitz efficient portfolios are likely to be dominated by other combinations of securities, and therefore suggested an alternative efficiency criterion, which restricts consideration to a subset of the Markowitz efficient frontier. As an example, it is supposed that portfolios C and D have the following expected returns and standard deviations of return.

	$E(R)(\%)$	$\sigma(\%)$
Portfolio C	8	1
Portfolio D	15	2

Neither of the above portfolios dominates the other according to the Markowitz criterion, since they do not possess identical expected returns or standard deviations, so they may both lie on the efficient frontier. However, if it is assumed that portfolio returns are normally distributed,* then it is 95 per cent certain that returns will be in the range $E(R) \pm 2\sigma$. We are therefore 97.5 per cent confident that the return on portfolio C will not exceed 10 per cent and also that the return on portfolio D will not be less than 11 per cent, so in general portfolio D will be preferred. Baumol suggested an efficiency criterion which is specifically designed to accommodate this type of situation, whereas the Markowitz model implies that an individual may well prefer portfolio C to portfolio D because of the lower risk level associated with the former. The modified criterion allows for different levels of risk aversion in that the individual may wish to be 68 per cent certain of obtaining a specific return $(E(R) \pm \sigma)$, 95 per cent certain $(E(R) \pm 2\sigma)$ and so on.

The reader will recall from chapter 1 that the main objection to the approach which Markowitz developed in the 1950s was the very large number of calculations which had to be performed. No fewer than 4,950 correlation coefficients were required for a portfolio of 100 securities. What was needed was a simplified method of balancing risk and return. We will see in the next chapter how Sharpe (1963) developed such a method.

---

* It has been shown empirically that returns are only approximately normally distributed. See, for example, Mandelbrot (1963) and Fama (1965).

International portfolio diversification

The return of a security purchased in the investor's domestic stock market comprises:

1 the capital appreciation of the asset over the period considered, and
2 the value of dividends received during the period.

The return of a security purchased in a foreign stock market, however, depends upon a third factor in addition to the capital gain and cash distribution elements:

3 the change in the relative value of the foreign currency expressed in terms of the investor's domestic currency.

The effects on risk and return of including assets denominated in foreign currency in the investor's portfolio are now considered.

When the investor is restricted to purchasing securities in his national stock market, his set of attainable portfolios is constrained by the securities available in that market. The efficient portfolios form a subset of this limited set of attainable portfolios. If international diversification of portfolios is permitted, the universe of securities is increased by all those securities available in foreign stock markets. The set of portfolios which the investor can attain also increases correspondingly. The crucial issue is whether the series of efficient portfolios corresponding to the international universe of securities differs from that series corresponding to the national universe. If the two sets of efficient portfolios correspond exactly, then nothing will be gained from international diversification. If the two sets differ, however, then some portfolios, attainable only when the purchase of securities in foreign capital markets is permitted, dominate portfolios which are efficient in the situation when purchases of securities are restricted to the investor's domestic capital market. In such cases, diversification of portfolios on an international scale yields benefits in that, for a given level of risk, the investor can increase his expected return as compared with the expected return from diversifying on a purely national scale, or alternatively, for a given level of expected return, can reduce risk.

It is interesting to investigate whether internationally diversified portfolios are likely to dominate those which are merely nationally diversified. In general, returns on securities for a given country are highly positively correlated, and equation (2.10) indicates that, as a result, the variance of return of nationally diversified portfolios is relatively high. If the correlations between returns of foreign securities and returns of domestic securities are lower than the correlations among returns of domestic securities, then gains should follow from diversifying portfolios internationally. Now, unlike returns on domestic securities, returns on foreign securities are subject to economic influences and government policies in foreign countries. In addition, returns on assets expressed in terms of foreign currency are affected by changes in exchange rates. As a result of these factors, correlations between returns of foreign securities and returns of domestic securities are likely to be relatively low, and so portfolios including foreign securities are likely to have lower variances of return than those comprising purely domestic securities. International diversification of portfolios should therefore be beneficial.

Grubel (1968) has extended the Markowitz model to internationally diversified asset holdings. He examines the potential gains to US investors from diversifying their portfolios internationally. He assumes that investors place their funds in securities which make up the common stock market indices of the countries included in his study. The monthly return obtained from such investment in each country is calculated for the period January 1959 to December 1966 by considering the capital gain, cash distribution and exchange rate elements (1, 2 and 3 respectively). These returns are used to compute the average rate of return and variance of return for each country and also the correlations among returns from the various countries. On substitution of these values into equations (2.6) and (2.10) it is possible to calculate the rates of return and variances of return of portfolios which include the available assets in different proportions. The efficient portfolios can then be computed. It is shown that, in general, international diversification of assets permits US investors to achieve higher rates of return or lower variances of return of portfolios compared with purely national diversification of assets. Grubel in fact derives two efficient sets of internationally diversified portfolios, one corresponding to an eight-country universe, and the other to an 11-country universe (these groups of countries are described in table 2.2). When attention is restricted to the eight-country universe, the increase in return attainable from international diversification is less than 20 per cent for the same level of risk as that applying to the US investment. On moving to the larger universe, however, the corresponding gain in return becomes almost 70 per cent. Substantial gains in welfare may therefore accrue to US investors if they diversify their portfolios internationally, particularly if the universe of securities is not confined to those available in the stock markets of Western Europe or North America. Grubel points out that the calculated gains from international diversification are biased upwards on account of two factors. First, he assumes that there are no additional risks attached to foreign as opposed to domestic investment other than changes in exchange rates, whereas in reality the possibility of war, confiscation or exchange restrictions increases the risk of investment abroad. The second problem is that transaction costs are likely to increase as the portfolio becomes more highly diversified, and these costs have been ignored in the analysis.

Levy and Sarnat (1970) also use the Markowitz model of portfolio choice to examine the potential benefits to US investors from international diversification of their portfolios. They assume investment in indices of common stocks and consider annual data on 28 countries for the period 1951 to 1967 (these countries are listed in table 2.2). The rate of return for each country is calculated as the

Table 2.2   Groups of countries considered in previous research

Grubel's 8-country universe	Grubel's 11-country universe	Levy and Sarnat's 28-country universe
Canada	As Grubel's 8 plus:	As Grubel's 11 plus:
US		Austria
Belgium	Australia	Denmark
France	Japan	Finland
Italy	South Africa	Norway
Netherlands		Sweden
West Germany		Portugal
UK		Spain
		Switzerland
		New Zealand
		Israel
		Ceylon
		India
		Chile
		Mexico
		Peru
		Philippines
		Venezuela

percentage change in the value of its index of common stocks expressed in terms of US dollars. Only the capital gain and exchange rate elements (1 and 2, respectively) are therefore used in the calculation. Hence the computed return is biased downwards as dividends are neglected. These return data are used to calculate the mean rate of return and variance of return for each country, and also the correlations among returns from the various countries. The set of efficient portfolios corresponding to the 28-country universe is calculated by Levy and Sarnat, who demonstrate that internationally diversified portfolios dominate those which are only diversified nationally. Examination of the composition of several of the efficient portfolios, however, shows that investment in the US accounts in each case for at least a third of total security holdings. Investment in Japan is also high, with combined US and Japanese investment comprising between 50 and 70 per cent of each efficient portfolio considered. Other countries featuring in all these portfolios are South Africa, Venezuela and Austria. The US investment enters the efficient portfolios on its own merits, as it is characterized by a relatively high rate of return and low risk. The rate of return on Japanese securities is also relatively high, but the variance of return is high. In spite of the latter defect, however, Japanese investment still forms a relatively large proportion of the efficient portfolios because the return on investment in Japanese securities is negatively correlated with the return on investment in US securities. Various subsets of the universe of 28 countries are also considered by Levy and Sarnat, and the corresponding sets of efficient portfolios computed. The authors show that if the US investor's portfolio consists of US securities only, then the rate of return on his investment is higher than if he restricts his portfolio entirely to the developing countries or Western Europe (at a comparable level of risk). Furthermore, whilst the US investor can marginally increase his rate of return (for the same level of risk) by diversifying his portfolio internationally so as to include investments in Canada and Western Europe as well as the US, it is only by widening the universe to include investments in Japan, South Africa and the developing countries that a substantial increase in the rate of return (for that level of risk) can be gained.

Viewed in isolation, foreign assets may appear unattractive to investors because of the additional element of risk (compared with domestic assets) caused by exchange rate fluctuations. When one reflects, however, that the risk of a portfolio depends not only upon the risk attached to each security included in the portfolio, but also upon the correlations among the returns of these securities, then it is clear that portfolios which are diversified internationally are likely to be superior to those which are merely diversified nationally. In other research, authors used data collected at different frequencies and for different time-periods, and considered different groups of countries, yet they obtained similar results. It was concluded, in each case, that if the US investor's portfolio consisted of North American and West European securities then he would be able to secure a modest increase in the rate of return compared with that obtained from purchasing US securities only (for the same level of risk). If the investor further diversified his portfolio to include investments in countries such as Japan and South Africa, it would be possible to obtain a substantial increase in the rate of return at the risk level associated with US investment. Although it is obviously beneficial for the US investor to purchase securities in countries outside North America and Western Europe, political considerations may deter him from some such investment. Furthermore, the risk of a portfolio is simply measured by the variance of its return, and other factors which in practice affect risk, such as the possibility of war, confiscation of assets, or exchange restrictions, are ignored. Certain investors may be unwilling to purchase assets in those countries which are 'risky' in terms of these non-quantified factors (for example some South American countries).

Research by Dimson, Hodges and Marsh (1980), using data for the period 1972–9, indicates similar benefits from international diversification for UK investors. The greatest risk reduction benefits tend to be obtained by UK investors diversifying into the stock markets of Japan and South Africa, rather than restricting foreign investment merely to the European and North American stock markets.

Conclusions

The Markowitz model constituted a major contribution to the problem of portfolio composition. It provided the foundation for the modern theory of portfolio management. Sharpe (1963) has developed a simplified version of the Markowitz formulation which overcomes the practical problems associated with the Markowitz technique – the substantial data requirements and computational burden. (Although the solutions obtained using the Sharpe model are only approximately efficient, Cohen and Pogue (1967) have demonstrated empirically that the model is reasonably accurate.) For example, in the 100-security universe case, the amount of data required is reduced from 5,150 for the full Markowitz model to 302 when the Sharpe simplification is incorporated, and fewer calculations are required. Sharpe's contribution is discussed in the next chapter.

Appendix

Axioms of rational investor behaviour

In order to define rational behaviour, the following notation is used, where x and y are events:

1 Strong-preference relationship.

$x > y$

x is strictly preferred to y.

2 Indifference relationship.

$x \sim y$

The individual is indifferent in a choice between x and y.

3 Weak-preference relationship.

$x \geq y$

x is strictly preferred to y, or the individual is indifferent in a choice between x and y.

4 Gamble.

$G(x, y : p)$

This denotes a gamble in which the outcome x occurs with probability p and the outcome y occurs with probability $1 - p$.

The behavioural assumptions which must be satisfied in order to be certain that individuals are 'rational' are as follows, where x, y, z and u are events.

Axiom 1: Comparability

Either $x > y$

or $y > x$

or $x \sim y$.

Axiom 2: Transitivity

If $x > y$ and $y > z$, then $x > z$.

If $x \sim y$ and $y \sim z$, then $x \sim z$.

This axiom is concerned with the concept of consistency of preferences.

Axiom 3: Strong independence

If $x \sim y$, then $G(x, z : p) \sim G(y, z : p)$.

If the individual is indifferent in a choice between x and y, then he will also be indifferent as regards a gamble set up between x with probability p and a mutually exclusive event z and another gamble set up between y with probability p and the mutually exclusive event z.

Axiom 4: Measurability

If $x > y \geqslant z$ or $x \geqslant y > z$

then there exists a unique p such that

$y \sim G(x, z : p)$.

If event y is preferred less than x but more than z, then there exists a unique probability p such that the individual will be indifferent in a choice between y and a gamble between x with probability p and z with probability $1 - p$.

Axiom 5: Ranking

If $x \geqslant y \geqslant z$ and $x \geqslant u \geqslant z$,

and also, if $y \sim G(x, z : p_1)$ and $u \sim G(x, z : p_2)$,

then if $p_1 > p_2$ this implies $y > u$,

or if $p_1 = p_2$ this implies $y \sim u$.

Given that an individual behaves in accordance with these axioms of rationality, and also that the marginal utility of wealth is always positive (that is, individuals always prefer more wealth to less), von Neumann and Morgenstern (1947) have shown that it is possible to derive a utility function (U) with the following properties:

1 If $U(x) > U(y)$, then $x > y$.

2 If $U(x) = U(y)$, then $x \sim y$.

3 $U[G(x, y : p)] = pU(x) + (1 - p) U(y)$.

The utility of a gamble is the weighted sum of the utilities of all possible outcomes, where the weights are the corresponding probabilities of occurrence.

Now the utility of a gamble is equivalent to expected utility. Furthermore, a given action may have many possible outcomes (defined in terms of resulting wealth). Hence

$$E[U(W)] = \sum_i p_i U(W_i)$$

where E denotes expected value, W denotes wealth and p_i denotes the probability that outcome i will occur. A rational individual chooses that action which maximizes his expected utility of wealth; that is, individuals behave as though they calculate the expected utility of wealth for all possible alternative actions, and then select that action which maximizes their expected utility of wealth.

Further reading

Copeland, T. E., and J. F. Weston: *Financial Theory and Corporate Policy*, London, Addison-Wesley, 1988, chapters 4 and 6.

Fama, E. F., and M. H. Miller: *The Theory of Finance*, London, Holt, Rinehart and Winston, 1972, chapter 5.

Markowitz, H. M.: Portfolio Selection. *Journal of Finance*, 7, March 1952, pp. 77–91.

Markowitz, H. M.: *Portfolio Selection: Efficient Diversification of Investments*, New York, John Wiley, 1959.

3

The capital asset pricing model

Assumptions

The major assumptions underlying the capital asset pricing model (CAPM) are as follows:

1 Investors base their portfolio investment decisions on the Markowitz expected return and standard deviation criteria.
2 Investors may borrow and lend without limit at the risk-free rate of interest.
3 Investors have homogeneous expectations about future outcomes over a one-period time horizon.
4 Capital markets are in equilibrium.
5 There are no market imperfections; investments are infinitely divisible, information is costless, there are no taxes, transaction costs or interest rate changes, and there is no inflation.

Some of these assumptions are obviously unrealistic, but they greatly simplify the model-building process. Furthermore, even if the assumptions are relaxed, it is likely that the CAPM may still hold approximately.

The market model

In order to identify the efficient set of portfolios in the Markowitz model, a huge quantity of data is required. In particular, it is necessary to know the covariance of return between each pair of securities in the asset universe. A major breakthrough in the practical utilization of portfolio theory came with Sharpe's (1963) development of the market (or single-index, or diagonal) model. This assumes that each security's price movement can be related to the price of the market portfolio – that is, a portfolio comprising a weighted average of all the securities traded on the market. Sharpe suggests that, in practice, a broad-based average, such as the *Financial Times* all-share index, may be used as a surrogate for the market index. The returns of the various securities in the asset universe are assumed to be related to each other only through common dependence upon this market index, and hence the necessity to specify the covariance of returns between every pair of securities is eliminated. This simplifying assumption results in a substantial reduction in the input requirements for the Markowitz model.

The market model generates a characteristic line by assuming that the return of a security is determined entirely by the market index and random factors:

$$R_i = \alpha_i + \beta_i R_M + U_i \tag{3.1}$$

where R_i is the return of the ith security, R_M is the return of the market portfolio, α_i and β_i are parameters, and U_i is a random error term. The error term is assumed to satisfy the usual properties required by the classical linear regression model: it has a mean of zero and finite variance; the error terms are independent of each other (that is, covariance $(U_i, U_j) = 0$ for all i and j, $i \neq j$); and R_M is independent of the error term (that is, covariance $(R_M, U_i) = 0$ for all i). The return of a security may therefore be split into two parts: that which is perfectly correlated with the market return (the systematic return) and that which is independent of the market return (the unsystematic return). Since the systematic return is perfectly correlated with the market return, it may be expressed as a factor β (beta) times the market return. The coefficient β_i therefore indicates the expected responsiveness of security i's return to changes in the level of the market index. The intercept term α (alpha) gives the expected return of the stock when the market return is zero, and represents the average value over time of the unsystematic returns of the security.

The market model equation (3.1) is illustrated graphically in figure 3.1. The intercept of the characteristic line on the vertical axis

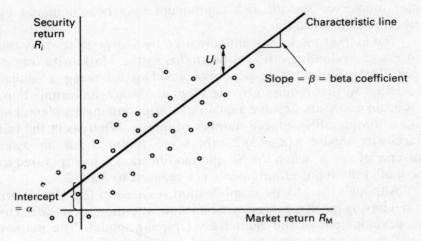

Figure 3.1   Characteristic line

is given by α_i, and the slope is given by β_i. The points represent a set of observations over time on the return of the security and the market return, and the vertical distance from any observation to the characteristic line is given by the error term. The market model may be fitted to these points by least-squares regression techniques, giving estimates of the parameters α_i and β_i.

The variance of a security may be broken down into its systematic and unsystematic components as follows:

$$V(R_i) = E[R_i - E(R_i)]^2 \tag{3.2}$$

where V denotes variance and E denotes expected value. On substitution from equation (3.1), this gives

$$V(R_i) = E[\alpha_i + \beta_i R_M + U_i - E(\alpha_i + \beta_i R_M + U_i)]^2$$
$$= E\{\beta_i[R_M - E(R_M)] + [U_i - E(U_i)]\}^2$$
$$= \beta_i^2 V(R_M) + V(U_i). \tag{3.3}$$

The first term on the right-hand side of equation (3.3) is the systematic (or market, or non-diversifiable) risk element. Systematic risk is the risk associated with the general performance of the stock market, and is determined by the variance of the market index and the magnitude of the parameter β_i. The second term on the right-hand side of equation (3.3) is the unsystematic (or specific, or diversifiable) risk element, which is unique to the ith security. This latter unique or specific risk component may be eliminated by sufficient diversification.

The market model was initially used by Sharpe to simplify the process of evaluating efficient portfolios in the Markowitz framework. Determining these portfolios involves following a similar procedure to that required by the original Markowitz formulation. It is again necessary to solve a quadratic programming problem, but with a considerably reduced number of inputs. Whereas in the full Markowitz model $n(n + 3)/2$ inputs are required for an asset universe of size n, when the Sharpe modification is incorporated in the model the input requirements are reduced to $3n + 2$.

Although the Sharpe simplification resulted in the Markowitz model having much greater practical value, attention soon shifted to the development of the capital asset pricing model. The market model provided the conceptual foundation for the CAPM; whereas the Markowitz model deals with the concept of total risk, the market model focuses on the concept of systematic risk as characterized by β.

Risk-free assets and the capital market line

The Markowitz mean-variance model may be modified by introducing into the analysis the concept of a risk-free asset. If it is assumed that the investor has access to risk-free securities (for example Treasury bills) in addition to the universe of risky securities, then he can construct a new set of portfolios as depicted by the line R_FM in figure 3.2. The risk-free asset may be combined with any portfolio on the efficient frontier to yield a new portfolio with characteristics determined by the proportions of each asset in the portfolio. The expected return and standard deviation of return of the new portfolio may be calculated as follows. Equation (2.7) states that the expected return of a two-asset portfolio, $E(R)$, is given by

$$E(R) = X_1\mu_1 + (1 - X_1)\mu_2$$

where X_1 is the proportion of security 1 in the portfolio, μ_1 is the expected return of security 1, and μ_2 is the expected return of security 2. Hence

$$E(R_p) = XE(R) + (1 - X)R_F \tag{3.4}$$

where $E(R_p)$ is the expected rate of return of the new portfolio, X is the proportion of the risky portfolio in the new portfolio, $E(R)$ is

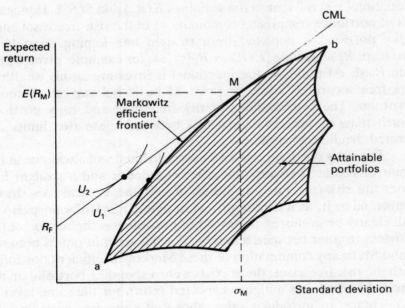

Figure 3.2 Capital market line

the expected return of the risky portfolio, and R_F is the risk-free rate of interest. Equation (2.11) states that the variance of a two-asset portfolio $V(R)$ is given by

$$V(R) = X_1^2\sigma_1^2 + (1 - X_1)^2\sigma_2^2 + 2X_1(1 - X_1)\rho_{12}\sigma_1\sigma_2$$

where σ_1^2 is the variance of return of security 1, σ_2^2 is the variance of return of security 2, and ρ_{12} is the correlation coefficient between the returns of securities 1 and 2. Thus

$$V(R_p) = X^2\sigma^2 \tag{3.5}$$

where $V(R_p)$ is the variance of return of the new portfolio, and σ^2 is the variance of return of the risky portfolio. The remaining terms on the right-hand side of equation (2.11) disappear, since the variance of return of the riskless asset is zero, as is the correlation of returns between the riskless asset and risky portfolio. The standard deviation of return of the new portfolio, $S(R_p)$, is therefore given by

$$S(R_p) = X\sigma. \tag{3.6}$$

Substituting for X in equation (3.4) from equation (3.6) yields

$$E(R_p) = R_F + \frac{E(R) - R_F}{\sigma} S(R_p). \tag{3.7}$$

Equation (3.7) is linear in the variables $E(R_p)$ and $S(R_p)$. Hence the set of portfolios comprising combinations of the risk-free asset and a risky portfolio is depicted by a straight line joining them, with intercept R_F and slope $[E(R) - R_F]/\sigma$, as, for example, given by the line R_FM. At point R_F the individual is investing all his wealth in risk-free securities, while at point M he is holding an all-equity portfolio. The combinations of risk-free asset and risky portfolio which may be achieved by points between these two limits are termed 'lending' portfolios.

The risky portfolio chosen by an individual will always be at the point of contact between the efficient frontier and a straight line from the risk-free rate of interest R_F on the vertical axis drawn tangential to it, as illustrated by M in figure 3.2. Risky portfolio M will clearly be preferred to any other portfolio on the section of the efficient frontier between a and M. For the array of points between a and M, or any combination of these Markowitz efficient portfolios with the risk-free asset, there exists a corresponding portfolio on the line R_FM which has a higher expected return for the same level of risk. Hence, by introducing the concept of a risk-free asset into the analysis, a new set of portfolios depicted by the line R_FM may be derived, which dominates the section of the Markowitz efficient frontier between a and M. The individual is therefore able to move to a higher level of utility than previously (for example from indifference curve U_1 to indifference curve U_2 in figure 3.2).

If the investor is able to borrow money at the same risk-free rate of interest, R_F, at which he can invest, then he can supplement his available wealth and construct a 'borrowing' portfolio. If the straight line joining R_F and M is extended to the right of point M, this section of the line represents borrowing portfolios (that is, portfolios in which the individual invests his available capital and an additional borrowed amount). As one moves further to the right of point M, an increasing amount of borrowed money is being invested. Clearly, the borrowing portfolios dominate the section of the Markowitz efficient frontier between M and b.

The straight line from R_F passing through point M shows the range of all possible portfolios in which the individual can invest by borrowing or lending at the risk-free rate of interest R_F and investing in the risky portfolio M. This line dominates the Markowitz efficient frontier, and is termed the capital market line (CML). The particular point chosen on the line will depend upon the individual's utility function, which will be determined by his attitude towards risk and expected return.

All investors will hold a portfolio on the CML – that is, a portfolio comprising some ratio of the risky portfolio M and the risk-free security. Hence portfolio M is the universally desired optimal portfolio, which must therefore contain all risky securities in proportions reflecting the total equity values of the companies they represent, and is known as the 'market' portfolio. Every security must enter the market portfolio in order to be traded, since all investors hold combinations of the market portfolio and the risk-free asset. Tobin (1958) thus derived a separation theorem which states that an investor's choice of risk level is completely independent of the problem of deriving the optimal portfolio of risky securities. The market portfolio represents the optimal combination of risky securities. Therefore, in choosing an efficient portfolio, all investors are directed towards the market portfolio. The risk level associated with the market portfolio may be too high or too low for an individual investor, and so he may hold a lending portfolio if he prefers lower risk and expected return than those of the market portfolio, or a borrowing portfolio if he prefers higher risk and expected return than those of the market portfolio. The decision to hold a lending or borrowing portfolio is, however, purely a financial decision based upon the investor's risk preference, and is completely independent of the investment decision to construct an efficient portfolio (that is, the market portfolio).

From equation (3.7) the capital market line is therefore:

$$E(R_p) = R_F + \frac{E(R_M) - R_F}{\sigma_M} S(R_p) \tag{3.8}$$

where $E(R_p)$ is the expected rate of return of any portfolio on the CML, R_F is the risk-free rate of interest, $E(R_M)$ is the expected rate of return of the market portfolio, σ_M is the risk (standard deviation of return) of the market portfolio, and $S(R_p)$ is the total risk (standard deviation of return) of a portfolio on the CML.

The expected rate of return from a portfolio on the CML thus comprises the risk-free rate of interest plus a risk premium. This premium is given by the market price of risk, $[E(R_M) - R_F]/\sigma_M$, multiplied by the risk of the portfolio. The CML depicts the expected return from perfectly diversified portfolios as a function of portfolio total risk.

The CML may be illustrated numerically as follows. It is supposed that

$$R_F = 8\%$$

$$E(R_M) = 14\%$$

$$\sigma_M = 10\%.$$

If three-quarters of an individual's wealth is invested in the risk-free security and one-quarter in the market portfolio (that is, he holds a lending portfolio), then from equation (3.4) the expected rate of return of the portfolio is

$$E(R_p) = 0.25 \times 0.14 + 0.75 \times 0.08$$

$$= 9.5\%.$$

From equation (3.6), the total portfolio risk is

$$S(R_p) = 0.25 \times 0.1$$

$$= 2.5\%.$$

Clearly, if the above value for $S(R_p)$ is substituted into the CML equation (3.8), this yields

$$E(R_p) = 0.08 + \frac{0.14 - 0.08}{0.1} \times 0.025$$

$$= 0.08 + 0.6 \times 0.025$$

$$= 9.5\%.$$

Now if the individual wishes to hold a borrowing portfolio, whereby he borrows 50 per cent of the value of his initial wealth to invest in the market portfolio in addition to all his available capital, equation (3.6) shows that the portfolio risk is

$$S(R_p) = 1.5 \times 0.1$$

$$= 15\%.$$

The expected return of such a portfolio is given by the CML equation (3.8) as

$$E(R_p) = 0.08 + 0.6 \times 0.15$$

$$= 17\%.$$

Thus, if an individual wishes to achieve expected return and risk levels below those corresponding to the market portfolio, he may invest in risk-free securities and the market portfolio. If he wishes to achieve expected return and risk levels higher than those of the market portfolio, he may borrow at the risk-free rate of interest and invest the proceeds plus his available wealth in the market portfolio.

The capital asset pricing model

Development of the CAPM

The CML equation (3.8) shows the return expected from any efficient portfolio. The problem now is to obtain the equation for the equilibrium expected return of an individual asset – that is, the one describing security market line (SML). The SML may be formally derived from the CML by analysing a portfolio comprising a risky security and the market portfolio in varying proportions. For a formal proof, see, for example, Sharpe (1964). An alternative formal derivation of the SML from the CML is given by Jensen (1972). We shall pursue a more intuitive derivation.

If the standard deviation of return is taken to measure risk, then from equation (3.3) the systematic risk of security i is equal to the β factor for the security multiplied by the standard deviation of the market return:

$$\text{security systematic risk} = \sigma_i^s$$

$$= \beta_i \sigma_M. \tag{3.9}$$

Since the term σ_M is common to all securities, it is often more convenient to think of the systematic risk of a security in relative terms, that is, merely in terms of its β value. The systematic risk of a portfolio is equal to the β factor for the portfolio, β_p, multiplied by the risk of the market index:

$$\text{portfolio systematic risk} = \sigma_p^s$$

$$= \beta_p \sigma_M. \tag{3.10}$$

Now the β factor of a portfolio is equal to a weighted average of those of the individual securities:

$$\beta_p = \sum_{i=1}^{n} X_i \beta_i \tag{3.11}$$

where X_i is the proportion of the market value of the portfolio invested in security i, and n is the number of securities in the portfolio. Hence the systematic risk of a portfolio is simply a weighted average of the systematic risk of the component securities.

The market portfolio is the sole example of a perfectly diversified risky portfolio. To hold individual risky securities or imperfectly diversified portfolios is inefficient because specific risk can be eliminated by further diversification. The prices of risky securities and their expected returns therefore compensate for market risk alone, since the market will not provide rewards for risk which can be eliminated. In an efficient market, securities with higher systematic risk should have higher expected returns, and those with the same systematic risk should have the same expected rate of return. The precise form of the relationship between risk and return is examined as follows.

Consider the case of an investor who holds a risky portfolio with $\beta = 1$. The expected rate of return of the portfolio is equal to the expected rate of return of the market portfolio. If a riskless portfolio is held (that is, a portfolio with $\beta = 0$) then the expected rate of return is the risk-free rate of interest. Suppose now that the individual invests a proportion X of his money in the risky portfolio and $(1 - X)$ in the riskless portfolio. From equation (3.11), the portfolio β is a weighted average of the β of the market portfolio and the β of the risk-free rate; that is,

$$\beta_p = (1 - X) \cdot 0 + X \cdot 1$$
$$= X. \tag{3.12}$$

The β of the composite portfolio is thus equal to the fraction of money invested in the risky portfolio. If 100 per cent or less of the investor's funds is invested in the risky portfolio, then $0 \leqslant \beta_p \leqslant 1$, but if he borrows at the risk-free rate of interest in order to invest in the risky portfolio, then $\beta_p > 1$. Now from equation (2.7), the expected return of the composite portfolio is also a weighted average of the expected returns of the two component portfolios:

$$E(R_p) = (1 - X)R_F + XE(R_M) \tag{3.13}$$

where $E(R_p)$ is the expected return of the composite portfolio, $E(R_M)$ is the expected return of the market portfolio, and R_F is the risk-free rate of interest. Substituting into equation (3.13) from equation (3.12) yields

$$E(R_p) = (1 - \beta_p)R_F + \beta_p E(R_M).$$

Therefore

$$E(R_p) = R_F + \beta_p[E(R_M) - R_F]. \tag{3.14}$$

Equation (3.14) is the capital asset pricing model (CAPM). This shows that there is a linear relationship between the expected return of a portfolio and the systematic risk of the portfolio (as measured by its β factor). When $\beta = 0$, the expected rate of return is equal to the risk-free rate of interest, but for risky investment ($\beta > 0$), the expected rate of return exceeds the risk-free rate of interest by an amount proportional to the market sensitivity (β) of the investment.

The CAPM may also be restated in 'risk-premium' form by subtracting the risk-free rate of interest from both sides of equation (3.14):

$$E(R_p) - R_F = \beta_p[E(R_M) - R_F]. \qquad (3.15)$$

In this form, the CAPM states that the expected portfolio risk premium (or excess return over the risk-free rate of interest) is equal to the portfolio β factor multiplied by the expected market risk premium (or excess return over the risk-free rate of interest).

A comparison of the CAPM and the market model

The market model for an individual security is given by equation (3.1). The corresponding market model for a portfolio is

$$R_p = \alpha_p + \beta_p R_M + U_p \qquad (3.16)$$

where R_p is the return of the portfolio, R_M is the return of the market index, α_p and β_p are parameters and U_p is a random error term. Equation (3.16) may be restated in risk-premium form as follows:

$$R_p - R_F = [\alpha_p - R_F(1 - \beta_p)] + \beta_p(R_M - R_F) + U_p. \qquad (3.17)$$

Comparing equations (3.16) and (3.17), it is clear that the slope of the line remains unchanged at β_p. The intercept term, however, changes from α_p in equation (3.16) to $[\alpha_p - R_F(1 - \beta_p)]$ in equation (3.17). From the market model (3.16), α_p may be interpreted as the expected return of the portfolio when the market return is zero. From equation (3.17), the risk-premium form of the market model, $[\alpha_p - R_F(1 - \beta_p)]$ may be interpreted as the portfolio expected risk premium (or expected excess return over the risk-free rate of interest) when the market return is equal to the risk-free rate of interest – that is, when the market risk premium (or excess return over the risk-free rate of interest) is zero. $[\alpha_p - R_F(1 - \beta_p)]$ is termed the 'risk-adjusted excess return'.

The risk-premium market model (3.17) may be rearranged to give

$$R_p = [\alpha_p - R_F(1 - \beta_p)] + R_F + \beta_p(R_M - R_F) + U_p. \qquad (3.18)$$

If the expectations operator is applied to equation (3.18), this yields

$$E(R_p) = [\alpha_p - R_F(1 - \beta_p)] + R_F + \beta_p[E(R_M) - R_F]. \quad (3.19)$$

The expectational market model (3.19) may be compared with the CAPM equation (3.14):

$$E(R_p) = R_F + \beta_p[E(R_M) - R_F].$$

It is clear that if a portfolio has a positive risk-adjusted excess return – that is, $\alpha_p > R_F(1 - \beta_p)$ – then its expected return is greater than that predicted by the CAPM; thus an investor holding a portfolio with a positive risk-adjusted excess return tends to beat the market. Similarly, if a portfolio has a negative risk-adjusted excess return – that is, $\alpha_p < R_F(1 - \beta_p)$ – then the expected return of the portfolio is less than that predicted by the CAPM; such a portfolio tends to underperform the market.

The market model (3.19) asserts that the risk-adjusted excess return may be positive, negative or zero. This model only reduces to the CAPM equation (3.14), however, when the risk-adjusted excess return is zero. Now the market model (3.17) is

$$R_p - R_F = [\alpha_p - R_F(1 - \beta_p)] + \beta_p(R_M - R_F) + U_p.$$

The characteristic line for the market portfolio reduces to

$$R_p - R_F = 0 + 1(R_M - R_F). \quad (3.20)$$

Equation (3.20) shows that $\{[\alpha_p - R_F(1 - \beta_p)] + U_p\} = 0$ for the market portfolio. The implications of this condition for security returns are as follows. Rewriting the market model (3.18) in terms of an individual security i yields

$$R_i = \{R_F + [\alpha_i - R_F(1 - \beta_i)] + U_i\} + \beta_i(R_M - R_F). \quad (3.21)$$

The first (bracketed) expression on the right-hand side of equation (3.21) represents the return of an investment in the non-market characteristics of security i, whereas the second term shows the return of an investment in the market characteristics of the security. If an individual borrows £β_i at the risk-free rate of interest, and invests this money in the market portfolio, his net return will be

$$\beta_i R_M - \beta_i R_F = \beta_i(R_M - R_F).$$

The second term on the right-hand side of equation (3.21) may therefore be viewed as the return of a financed investment in the market portfolio, and so an investment of £1 in any security may be split into the component parts:

(1) £1 invested in the non-market characteristics of the security, and
(2) £β_i borrowed at the risk-free rate of interest and then invested in the market portfolio.

The return associated with the latter component of investment in a security should be the same as an explicit investment in the market portfolio. In order to determine the return expected from investment in the non-market characteristics of the security, it is necessary to recall that for the market portfolio $\{[\alpha_p - R_F(1 - \beta_p)] + U_p\} = 0$, so the return of an investment in the non-market characteristics of the market portfolio is the risk-free rate of interest. Now in an efficient market all securities are priced correctly. Furthermore, the unsystematic risk associated with any security may be eliminated by holding a completely diversified portfolio – the market portfolio – so no reward should be expected for accepting unsystematic risk. Thus the return expected from investment in the non-market characteristics of the security is the risk-free rate of interest; that is,

$$E\{[\alpha_i - R_F(1 - \beta_i)] + U_i\} = 0.$$

Therefore

$$\alpha_i - R_F(1 - \beta_i) = 0. \tag{3.22}$$

Hence, in an efficient market, all securities are priced so that the risk-adjusted excess return is zero, and thus the risk-adjusted excess return of any given portfolio must also be zero. The market model (3.19) therefore reduces to the CAPM equation (3.14) in an efficient market.

Individual securities and the security market line

The characteristic line for an individual security is given by equation (3.21):

$$R_i = R_F + [\alpha_i - R_F(1 - \beta_i)] + U_i + \beta_i(R_M - R_F).$$

In an efficient market $[\alpha_i - R_F(1 - \beta_i)] = 0$ (equation (3.22)).

Substituting this condition into equation (3.21) and taking expected values gives

$$E(R_i) = R_F + \beta_i[E(R_M) - R_F]. \tag{3.23}$$

Equation (3.23) represents the security market line (SML), and shows that the expected return of a security is a linear function of the β factor of the security. Thus, for a correctly priced security, there is a linear relationship between expected return and systematic risk.

Equation (3.23) may be rearranged to give the risk-premium form of the SML as follows:

$$E(R_i) - R_F = \beta_i[E(R_M) - R_F]. \tag{3.24}$$

In this form, the SML states that the expected excess return of security i is equal to the security's β factor multiplied by the expected market excess return. Thus, for a correctly priced security, there is a linear relationship between expected excess return and systematic risk.

Since unsystematic risk may be eliminated by diversification, it is only necessary to accept market risk. A security's contribution to market risk, as measured by its β factor, is thus the relevant part of its overall risk. Furthermore, all correctly priced securities lie on the SML, and so do all portfolios of correctly priced securities. Therefore, in an efficient market, for all securities and all portfolios of securities, there is a linear relationship between expected return (or expected excess return) and risk.

The SML equation (3.23) is illustrated graphically in figure 3.3. The intercept of the SML on the vertical axis is given by the risk-free rate of interest R_F, and the slope is given by $[E(R_M) - R_F]$, the market risk premium – that is, the expected excess return of the market portfolio. Point M denotes the market portfolio, and here the expected return is $E(R_M)$ and the β factor equals unity.

The SML equation (3.24) is shown graphically in figure 3.4. In this case the SML goes through the origin, but the slope again measures the market risk premium. Point M represents the market portfolio, and here the expected excess return is $[E(R_M) - R_F]$ and the β value is unity.

The expected rate of return of an individual security for which $\beta = 1$ is equal to the expected rate of return of the market portfolio. If $\beta = 0.5$ for a particular security, then a 1 per cent increase (or decrease) in the expected market return results in a 0.5 per cent

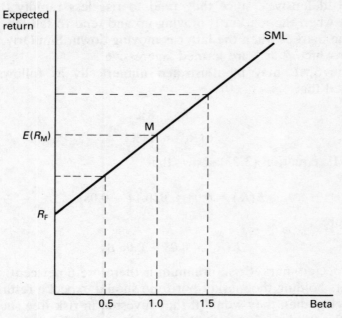

Figure 3.3 Security market line

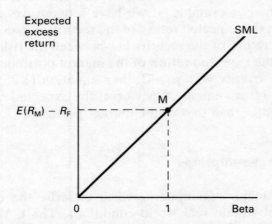

Figure 3.4 Security market line: risk-premium form

increase (or decrease) in the expected return of the security; this is a low-risk security. If $\beta = 2$ for a given security, then a 1 per cent increase (or decrease) in the expected market return results in a 2 per cent increase (or decrease) in the expected return of the security; such a security is high-risk. Securities for which $\beta < 1$ are termed 'defensive', since they tend to rise less rapidly than the market when the market is moving up and tend to fall less rapidly than the market when the latter is moving down. Similarly, securities for which $\beta > 1$ are termed 'aggressive'.

The SML may be illustrated numerically as follows. It is supposed that

$$R_F = 8\%$$

$$E(R_M) = 14\%.$$

The SML equation (3.23) shows that

$$E(R_i) = 0.08 + \beta_i(0.14 - 0.08).$$

Therefore

$$E(R_i) = 0.08 + 0.06\,\beta_i. \tag{3.25}$$

The expected market risk premium is therefore 6 per cent: that is, investors holding the market portfolio should expect a return 6 per cent higher than they would if they invested in risk-free securities. Given the β value of an individual security or portfolio of securities, equation (3.25) may be used to calculate the corresponding expected return. For example, if we have a defensive security with $\beta = 0.5$, then the expected return of the security equals 11 per cent; the expected return of the security lies between the risk-free rate of interest and the expected return of the market portfolio. If we have an aggresive security with $\beta = 2$, then equation (3.25) shows that the expected return equals 20 per cent; the expected return of the security is higher than that of the market portfolio.

Relaxing the assumptions

Most of the major assumptions which underlie the capital asset pricing model violate real world conditions. The CAPM may be expanded by relaxing the assumptions in order to determine the effect of more realistic assumptions. The impact of relaxing certain assumptions is now examined.

Different lending and borrowing rates

It is highly improbable that an investor will be able to borrow and lend at the same rate of interest. The more realistic situation in which the borrowing rate is higher than the lending rate is therefore examined.

The implications of differential lending and borrowing rates may be seen by re-examining the capital market line diagram. Figure 3.5 shows the new situation. If R_F is the risk-free rate of interest at which funds can be lent, then the straight line from R_F drawn tangentially to the Markowitz efficient frontier at P_L constitutes the efficient boundary up to P_L. The line $R_F P_L$ dominates all points on the risky-asset efficient frontier to the left of P_L. If R_B is the rate of interest at which funds can be borrowed, where $R_B > R_F$, then the optimal risky-asset portfolio in which to invest borrowed funds is given by P_B, the point at which a straight line from R_B is tangential to the Markowitz efficient frontier. Hence, that part of the line from R_B passing through point P_B which is situated to the right of P_B dominates all points on the risky-asset efficient frontier to the right of P_B. Thus if the individual requires an expected return–risk combination which is less than or equal to $E(R_L):S(R_L)$, he will choose a point on the line $R_F P_L$. Similarly, if he requires an expected return–risk combination which is greater than or equal to $E(R_B):S(R_B)$, the investor will choose a point to the

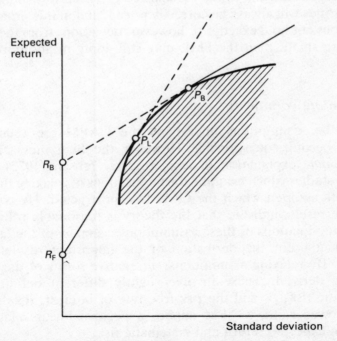

Figure 3.5   Capital market line: different lending and borrowing rates

right of P_B situated on the line from R_B passing through P_B. If, however, the individual wishes to select an expected return–risk combination which lies between $E(R_L){:}S(R_L)$ and $E(R_B){:}S(R_B)$, he will have to select a portfolio on the Markowitz efficient frontier between P_L and P_B, since all portfolios on the original efficient frontier between these two points remain undominated. Thus, if different lending and borrowing rates are permitted, a unique market portfolio no longer exists, since any of the risky portfolios between P_L and P_B may be selected.

As there is no unique market portfolio, the CML is no longer a straight line. Furthermore, since the security market line is derived from the CML, the SML relationships (3.23) and (3.24) cease to hold exactly. The explanatory power of the CAPM theory is therefore reduced when different lending and borrowing rates are introduced, although the theory may still hold approximately.

Disequilibrium in capital markets

In general, capital markets are in a state of disequilibrium. For example, changing expectations as a result of new information leads to continuous shifting within the market. It is therefore unlikely that all securities will always be correctly priced, and in this situation the SML does not hold exactly. If, however, deviations from the correct price are small, then the SML may still apply in an approximate sense.

Concluding comments

When the assumptions underlying the CAPM are relaxed, its validity becomes questionable. However, the theory may still be an *approximate* explanation of asset pricing. Jensen (1972) reports various studies which examine the implications of relaxing the major assumptions upon which the CAPM is constructed. He concludes that the results indicate that the theory is reasonably robust with regard to violations of these assumptions, as many of the latter are not essential for the derivation of the important results of the CAPM. By relaxing assumptions, alternative forms of the CAPM may be derived. These involve slightly different definitions of systematic risk, β, and the risk-free rate of interest, R_F. In every case, however, the CAPM implies a positive linear relationship between expected return and systematic risk.

As the important results of the CAPM still hold when more realistic assumptions than those underlying the original model are present, the CAPM is likely to be a reasonable approximation to the manner in which securities are actually priced in capital markets. Indeed, although the *simplest* form of the CAPM may not yield a completely adequate explanation of security returns, empirical studies by Jensen and Scholes (1972) and Blume and Friend (1973) have shown that securities with high β values tend to yield correspondingly high expected rates of return. Furthermore, Fama and MacBeth (1973) have demonstrated empirically that the relationship between expected return and β is linear.

Measurement of portfolio performance

The returns of managed portfolios, such as unit trusts, may be judged relative to the returns of unmanaged portfolios at the same level of risk using the CAPM. If the return of a managed portfolio exceeds the corresponding return of an unmanaged portfolio (the 'performance standard'), then the portfolio manager has beaten the market – he has performed in a superior manner. Similarly, if the return of a managed portfolio is less than the return of the performance standard, then the portfolio manager has underperformed the market.

The 'benchmark' portfolios against which the performance of managed portfolios may be evaluated are merely combinations of the risk-free asset and the market index. The reader will recall that the CAPM equation (3.14) is

$$E(R) = R_F + \beta_p[E(R_M) - R_F]$$

where $E(R)$ is the expected return of a portfolio with risk factor β_p, $E(R_M)$ is the expected return of the market portfolio, and R_F is the risk-free rate of interest. The above equation is stated in terms of investors' expectations rather than in terms of realized returns. If, however, realized returns are observed over a reasonably large number of periods and average realized returns calculated, then the following relationship holds approximately:

$$\bar{R} = \bar{R}_F + \beta_p(\bar{R}_M - \bar{R}_F) \tag{3.26}$$

where $\bar{R}$, $\bar{R}_M$ and $\bar{R}_F$ are the (arithmetic) average, realized, rates of return of the portfolio, the market and the risk-free asset. Thus the return of the performance standard for a managed portfolio with risk factor β_p is given by

$$\bar{R}_S = \bar{R}_F + \beta_p(\bar{R}_M - \bar{R}_F) \tag{3.27}$$

where $\bar{R}_S$ is the average realized rate of return of the performance standard. If $\bar{R}_p$ denotes the (arithmetic) average realized rate of return of the managed portfolio, then the portfolio manager's performance may be measured by

$$\bar{\alpha}_p^* = \bar{R}_p - \bar{R}_S. \tag{3.28}$$

Managed portfolios for which $\bar{\alpha}_p^*$ is positive have outperformed the standard, and those for which $\bar{\alpha}_p^*$ is negative have underperformed the standard. Of course, the CAPM assumes that $E(\bar{R}_p) = E(\bar{R}_S)$, that is, $E(\bar{\alpha}_p^*) = 0$.

The return of the managed portfolio is given by the market model (3.18):

$$R_p = [\alpha_p - R_F(1 - \beta_p)] + R_F + \beta_p(R_M - R_F) + U_p.$$

If realized returns are observed over a reasonably large number of periods and average realized returns calculated, then the following market model relationship holds approximately:

$$\bar{R}_p = [\alpha_p - \bar{R}_F(1 - \beta_p)] + \bar{R}_F + \beta_p(\bar{R}_M - \bar{R}_F). \tag{3.29}$$

Subtracting equation (3.27) from equation (3.29) gives

$$\bar{R}_p - \bar{R}_S = \alpha_p - \bar{R}_F(1 - \beta_p). \tag{3.30}$$

Thus

$$\bar{\alpha}_p^* = \alpha_p - \bar{R}_F(1 - \beta_p), \tag{3.31}$$

or

$$\alpha_p^* = \alpha_p - R_F(1 - \beta_p). \tag{3.32}$$

Now in our earlier discussion of the market model, $[\alpha_p - R_F(1 - \beta_p)]$ was termed the 'risk-adjusted excess return'. Hence, a managed portfolio with a positive estimated risk-adjusted excess return has beaten the performance standard, whereas one with a negative value has underperformed the standard.

A critique of the capital asset pricing model

Roll (1977) criticizes capital asset pricing theory testing as follows. First, he points out that the only testable hypothesis associated with the theory is whether or not the market portfolio is mean-variance efficient. If it is efficient, then the other implications of the CAPM, in particular the linear relationship between expected return and risk, follow as a direct consequence. Secondly, in empirical testing a proxy measure must be used for the market portfolio, but unless the market portfolio can be identified exactly (or a portfolio where the returns are perfectly correlated with those of the market portfolio), it is impossible to accept or reject the CAPM. Any proxy might or might not be mean-variance efficient, but this would not prove or disprove the presumed linear relationship between expected return and risk. The Roll critique, therefore, implies that tests of the CAPM should be interpreted with great caution.

The use of the CAPM in evaluating the performance of portfolio managers has also been criticized by Roll (1980). In this situation, the return of a managed portfolio is compared with that of an unmanaged portfolio at the same level of risk. Roll argues that using a proxy for the market portfolio (for example the *Financial Times* all-share index) as a benchmark for assessing performance is invalid. Since a market proxy may not lie on the efficient frontier (that is, may not be mean-variance efficient) it is impossible to deduce whether or not the risk-adjusted excess returns measured with reference to such an index are indeed attributable to a portfolio manager's investment ability, or merely follow as a result of using an inefficient market index. Furthermore, Roll shows that if the performance of two managed portfolios is compared using different market proxies, the rankings of the risk-adjusted excess returns (that is, performance) may be reversed.

Errors in performance measurement may be caused by random variation and the *ex ante* CAPM benchmark. Whereas errors attributable to random causes tend to be eliminated by repeated evaluations, this is not the case with benchmark errors. Thus, if an investment manager happens to choose a portfolio with negative benchmark error, he will appear to beat the market, while if a portfolio has positive benchmark error it will appear to under-perform the market. Roll first considers the situation in which the appropriate risk level of a portfolio is inaccurately assessed. This occurs if the chosen market index is inefficient, and the error is the difference between the calculated value of β and that which would have been obtained using an efficient index. An inaccurate assessment of risk causes true performance to differ from measured performance, as illustrated in figure 3.6. Performance is measured by the difference between the observed return of the portfolio and that predicted by the security market line. At the incorrectly assessed risk level, $\hat{\beta}_p$, the portfolio manager appears to have outperformed the market because the observed return, R_p, lies above that predicted by the SML, $E(\hat{R}_s)$: the measured performance $\hat{\alpha}_p^* = R_p - E(\hat{R}_s)$ is positive. The true risk associated with the portfolio is larger than the measured risk, however, and at the true risk level, β_p, the expected return, $E(R_s)$, lies above the observed return, so the actual performance is negative and equal to $(-\alpha_p^*) = R_p - E(R_s)$. Roll then considers the case in which true and measured performances differ because the position of the SML is incorrect. This may happen either because an inefficient market index has been employed – that is, an index where the expected return, $E(\hat{R}_M)$, differs from that of a mean-variance efficient market index, $E(R_M)$ – or because the return of the nominal 'risk-free' asset used, $\hat{R}_F$, differs from that of the true risk-free asset, $\overline{R}_F$. Such a situation is depicted in figure 3.7. Here again, the measured performance is positive and equal to $\hat{\alpha}_p^* = R_p - E(\hat{R}_s)$, whereas in fact the true performance is negative and equal to $(-\alpha_p^*) = R_p - E(R_s)$. The error between true performance and estimated perfor-

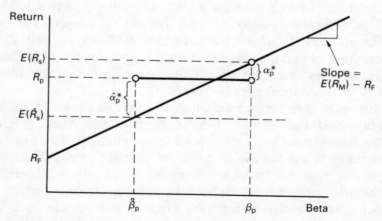

Figure 3.6   Incorrect evaluation of performance caused by inaccurate assessment of portfolio risk level

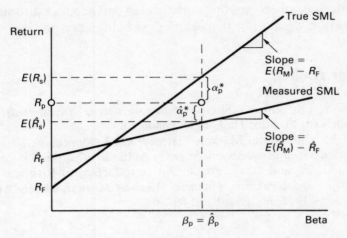

Figure 3.7   Incorrect evaluation of performance caused by incorrect positioning of security market line

mance may therefore be caused by inaccurate assessment of any of the three components of the SML – the β coefficient, the expected return of the market index, or the risk-free rate of interest. Roll demonstrates, however, that in each case the critical ingredient determining whether true performance and measured performance differ is the optimality or non-optimality of the chosen market index (that is, whether or not the chosen index is mean-variance efficient). CAPM benchmark error is thus present whenever the market index is not an *ex ante* mean-variance efficient portfolio, and this error will not average out over repeated manager evaluations.

Although Roll has highlighted some of the problems associated with the CAPM, the only practical alternative to using a widely recognized and broad market index (such as the *Financial Times* all-share index) is to cease completely to attempt to measure risk-adjusted relative performance. Furthermore, Mayers and Rice (1978) have refuted Roll's critique to the extent that they have shown that under fairly general conditions portfolio performance tests using the CAPM can give meaningful results. Hence, provided that the chosen index comprises a high proportion of the total market value of securities, it would appear to be an acceptable basis for calculating β values and for performance measurement judgements. Despite the imperfections of capital asset pricing theory, the CML benchmarks can provide useful information regarding the performance of competing investment managers, although the information should not be regarded as being very precise.

Further reading

Alexander, G., and W. Sharpe: *Fundamentals of Investments*, Hemel Hempstead, Prentice Hall, 1989, chapter 8.

Jensen, M. C.: Capital Markets: Theory and Evidence. *Bell Journal of Economics and Management Science*, Autumn 1972, pp. 357–98.

Modigliani, F., and G. A. Pogue: An Introduction to Risk and Return Concepts and Evidence. *Financial Analysts Journal*, March–April and May–June 1974, pp. 68–80 and 69–86.

4

The efficient market hypothesis: the early evidence

Introduction

The efficient market hypothesis (EMH) suggests that, at any point in time, share prices fully reflect all information, any new or shock information being immediately incorporated into the share price. To the extent that the hypothesis holds in the real world, it has powerful implications for investment management, which are discussed later, in chapter 5. In this chapter we identify the three forms in which the hypothesis has generally been tested, and briefly summarize a few of the many studies of market efficiency. Tests of the EMH are classified as weak form tests, semi-strong form tests and strong form tests. The EMH is generally supported by all three kinds of test, but there is some strong form evidence of market inefficiency which gives encouragement to professional portfolio managers to seek out underpriced securities.

The weak form of the efficient market hypothesis suggests that future prices cannot be predicted from past price data. Share prices have no memory. Successive price changes are independent. Any implications from historic events for future share prices are already reflected in today's price. Only new or shock information will cause prices to change, but new information cannot be predicted. This 'random walk' or sub-martingale version of the EMH is supported by many studies, including those by Bachelier (1900), Working (1934), Kendall (1953), Roberts (1959), Osborne (1959), Alexander

(1961), Cootner (1962), Granger and Morgenstern (1963), Moore (1964), Fama (1965), Samuelson (1965) and Niederhoffer and Osborne (1966).

The semi-strong version suggests that share prices fully reflect all publicly available information. Prices adjust instantaneously to such new information as is contained in earnings announcements, stock splits, dividend announcements and large block trades. It is therefore not possible to use such public information to make excess returns. Again, a great many studies support the hypothesis, including those by Ball and Brown (1968), Fama, Fisher, Jensen and Roll (1969), Kaplan and Roll (1972), Scholes (1972) Kraus and Stoll (1972), Pettit (1972), Sunder (1973) and Mandelker (1974).

Finally, the strong form of the EMH suggests that share prices fully reflect all information, even information which is not publicly available. This is indeed a strong version, because it suggests that even market professionals, who study companies very carefully and devote a great deal of time to the fundamental analysis of a company's worth, cannot achieve excess returns. Many studies support the hypothesis by examining the performance of unit trust/mutual fund managers. The good news for portfolio managers is that there is some evidence that the hypothesis does not hold absolutely at the strong form level. There have been many studies of the strong form of the EMH, including those by Friend, Brown, Herman and Vickers (1962), Sharpe (1966), Jensen (1968), Friend, Blume and Crockett (1970) and Firth (1978). Evidence against the strong form is provided by Niederhoffer and Osborne (1966), Scholes (1972), Jaffe (1974), Ambachtsheer (1974) and Dimson and Marsh (1984). We emphasize that we provide only a few summaries of the great number of research studies published to date.

Weak form tests of the EMH

Bachelier (1900)

As long ago as 1900, Louis Bachelier concluded that the price of a commodity today is the best estimate of its price in the future. Commodity speculation is apparently a fair game in which neither buyers nor sellers should expect to make profits. In such a competitive market, prices tend to follow a random walk.

Working (1934)

The random behaviour of commodity prices was again noted by Holbrook Working during the 1930s in an analysis of time series data.

Kendall (1953)

In another, later, study, Maurice Kendall attempted to find cycles in indices of security and commodity prices. To his surprise, no cycles could be found. Prices today appear to be yesterday's price plus some random change. He suggested that prices appear to follow a random walk, each price change being independent of previous price changes.

Roberts (1959)

In 1959, Roberts demonstrated that a series of cumulative random numbers has the same visual appearance as a time series of share prices. An observer can in fact see patterns in share prices with hindsight, but the series is randomly generated. Roberts also demonstrated that changes in the numbers generated randomly have the same visual appearance as changes in share prices. The tentative conclusion is that share prices appear to follow a random walk.

Osborne (1959)

A second study in 1959 is provided by Osborne. He examined share prices with a view to discovering whether or not their movements conformed with a law of physics. The movement of very small particles suspended in solution is known to physicists as 'Brownian motion'. Osborne found a high degree of conformity between movements in share prices and the law governing Brownian motion. The variance of price changes over successively longer intervals of time increases in accordance with the square of the length of time. This implies that the logarithms of price changes are independent of each other. A market in which successive price changes are independent of each other is a random walk market.

Alexander (1961)

The suggestion that share prices appeared to follow a random walk was not popular with those stock market professionals who offered advice on individual security selection. In 1961, Alexander attempted to show that historic price movements could be used to earn abnormal returns. He used a filter technique, suggesting purchase of a share if its price increases by a percentage over its previous low, and suggesting disposal if the price falls by a set percentage from a previous high. At first, the filter technique appeared to produce exceptionally high returns. However, when transaction costs were taken into account the excess gains disappeared. The results were interesting because short trends were apparent in share price movements, although the trends were so short that any exploitation was cancelled by transaction costs.

Cootner (1962)

In this article, Cootner argues that stock markets do appear to be random walks for most people. However, professional investors can observe the random walks in security prices produced by non-professional market participants, until the price wanders sufficiently far away from the intrinsic or fundamental value of the security. At this point, the professionals can trade in such a way as to make abnormal returns. If professional investment managers could identify overpriced and underpriced securities in this way, then they would help to stabilize stock market prices, and consistently achieve abnormal returns. As will be indicated shortly, the strong form tests of the EMH find only occasional evidence of superior performance by market professionals.

Granger and Morgenstern (1963)

In 1963, Granger and Morgenstern used spectral analysis in an attempt to find cycles in share prices. Spectral analysis seeks out more complex relationships than can be identified by the simple serial correlation technique generally adopted by other studies. No significant relationship was found between security returns in one period and security returns in previous periods. This study provides further support for the notion that security price movements follow a random walk.

Moore (1964)

Moore was one researcher examining serial correlation between successive price changes in individual securities. A low correlation coefficient suggests that previous price changes cannot be used to predict future changes. For weekly price changes of 29 stocks during the period 1951–8, he found an average serial correlation coefficient of −0.06. As this is not significantly different from zero, it appears that historic weekly price changes cannot be used to predict future price changes.

Fama (1965)

In a major study conducted by Fama, the average serial correlation coefficient, of 0.03, was again not significantly different from zero. The data were the proportionate daily price changes of the 30 industrial stocks making up the Dow-Jones Industrial Average for the five years ending in 1962. Fama also investigated the phenomenon of price changes in the same direction. Such an analysis of runs attempts to determine whether there is any dependency between successive price changes. The conclusion is that there is very little evidence of dependence. Historical price information provides little, if any, information which can be used to achieve abnormal returns.

Samuelson (1965)

Samuelson provides additional evidence in support of stock markets complying at least with the weak form of the efficient market hypothesis. He proves that prices will move in a random manner in a market in which all investors have similar time horizons and expectations, providing that all information is available to all market participants at zero cost. Of course, we should not expect all the conditions to hold absolutely, but we would expect highly competitive and active stock markets, such as exist in London and New York, to comply sufficiently with these conditions for the pricing mechanism to be very efficient, at least in the weak form.

Niederhoffer and Osborne (1966)

Some slight evidence of runs and reversals is provided by Niederhoffer and Osborne in a study of insider trading. We might expect prices at t to be completely independent of prices at $t - 1$, but this study shows that during the course of a day price changes are correlated to some extent, and that the changes are negatively correlated, the correlation coefficient being -0.25. This information is available to the specialist dealing in securities, and can therefore be used by him in making trading decisions. The phenomenon of insider trading will be referred to again as evidence of strong form inefficiency.

Semi-strong form tests of the EMH

The weak form tests generally suggest that historic price movements cannot be used to forecast future prices. The semi-strong version of the EMH suggests that share prices reflect all publicly available information. If the hypothesis holds in the real world, then it is not possible to achieve abnormal returns by studying accounting numbers, dividend announcements, earnings announcements, stock splits, or merger announcements.

Ball and Brown (1968)

This study uses monthly data for 261 companies for the period 1946–65 in an investigation into the usefulness of earnings published in annual accounts. Are earnings anticipated? Should we expect share prices to swing wildly on the announcement of a company's annual earnings? In the Ball and Brown study, estimates are made of the stock market's forecast annual earnings. The share price reaction to the actual earnings announcement is then studied. Good news should result in a share price increase, and bad news in a decrease. The sample of companies is divided into two groups – those having earnings higher than expected and those having earnings lower than expected. Those companies having higher than expected returns offer abnormally high returns 12 months in advance of the announcement. Returns adjust gradually during the 12-month period until the date of the announcement. By this date, just about all the necessary adjustment has taken place. The market has anticipated the good news, and prices have adjusted accordingly. The same is true for companies achieving lower earnings than expected. The market price adjusts during the 12 months up to the date of the announcement, by which time just about all the necessary adjustment has occurred. Market prices adjust during the year, as information becomes publicly available in interim reports, brokers' forecasts, and newspaper coverage. Approximately 90 per cent of the content of annual reports is publicly available before the annual accounts are published. The study supports the semi-strong version of the EMH, in that the market anticipates economic events. Abnormal returns cannot be made by reacting to publicly available information, which is either anticipated or immediately incorporated into the share price. It is not possible to achieve abnormal returns once information becomes publicly available.

Fama, Fisher, Jensen and Roll (1969)

Are shareholders fooled by stock splits? Is there any bonus in a bonus share? Fama, Fisher, Jensen and Roll used data for 30 months before and 30 months after the stock split date for 940 stock splits between 1927 and 1959. Positive abnormal returns were found to occur before, but not after, the date of the split. Are the abnormal returns caused by the split? They should not be, because the owner of 1 per cent of a company's anticipated future cash flows still owns 1 per cent after the split or bonus issue. There is no bonus in a bonus issue. The split, however, might convey economic information about future cash flows. Higher cash flows might result in higher dividends. The researchers formulated the hypothesis that the split would convey economic information relating to future dividends. The sample was divided into those companies which subsequently increased their dividends beyond the market average, and those which did not. After the date of the split, small positive abnormal returns were associated with those companies which did increase dividends beyond the average, whereas falls in cumulative average residuals were associated with those companies which apparently failed to meet the expectation of higher dividends. Fama, Fisher, Jensen and Roll, therefore, present evidence consistent with the semi-strong form of market efficiency. Share prices reflect anticipated cash flows. Shareholders are not fooled by stock splits. The stock split is important only in so far as it conveys economic information. Share prices react in an unbiased manner to economic events. Stock splits are publicly available information. No abnormal returns should be expected after their announcement.

Kaplan and Roll (1972)

Is it possible for companies to fool investors by changes in accounting policies? Reported profits can be manipulated by the accounting treatment of depreciation, stock valuation, research and development, accrued income, accrued expenditure, government grants, and transfers to reserves. Kaplan and Roll investigated the impact of changes in depreciation policy on share prices. The change does not affect cash flow or the amount of corporation tax payable. In the UK, capital allowances are granted for tax purposes; accounting depreciation charges are not. The study found that, for the sample of 71 firms, there was no evidence that increasing earnings per share by reducing depreciation charges had any permanent positive effect on the value of the firm. Apparently, shareholders quite rationally discount cash flows, not earnings per share. The same researchers examined the effect of a different accounting treatment of a government tax credit. This also had no effect on cash flow. In such cases, shareholders might perhaps be fooled temporarily, but the effect was not permanent.

Scholes (1972)

In 1972, Scholes examined the effect of secondary offerings (large block trades) on security prices. He used daily returns on 345 secondary offerings between 1961 and 1965. These large block trades are associated with a very small price decline, but the amount of the decline does not depend on the amount of the disposal, it depends on the 'quality' of the seller. The largest declines follow disposals by corporations and officers of corporations (corporate insiders), investment companies and unit trusts. The market apparently suspects that these disposers have inside information. Much smaller declines are associated with disposals by banks, insurance companies, individuals and trustees. Again, it appears to be the information content of the disposal which is more important than the amount of the disposal.

Kraus and Stoll (1972)

Kraus and Stoll studied the effect on security prices of all block trades of 10,000 shares or more on the New York Stock Exchange between July 1968 and September 1969. Like Scholes, they found an effect on share price associated with large block trades. Large block disposals lead to a decrease in share price, but the price recovers very quickly and substantially by the end of the day. The day after the block trade, there is no predictable price reaction; the market apparently absorbs large deals very well. It is not possible to make abnormal returns by using publicly available information relating to block trades.

Pettit (1972)

In 1972, Pettit examined the reaction of the market to dividend announcements. As the dividend announcement is publicly available information, we should not be surprised by the results of the study. There is no evidence that security prices are affected following a firm's dividend announcement. The information content of dividends is immediately reflected in share prices. This is entirely consistent with the semi-strong form of market efficiency.

Sunder (1973)

In this study, Sunder examines the effect on stock market valuation of firms switching to a last-in, first-out (LIFO) method of stock valuation. Charging goods to production at the latest costs would tend to reduce taxable profits. Quite rationally, share prices increase as investors anticipate the change. After the change, no abnormal price reaction is observed. A change in stock valuation may lead to a fall in earnings per share, but not to a fall in the value of shares. Again, shareholders quite rationally discount cash flows, not accounting profit. Efficient capital markets anticipate events, so abnormal returns cannot be made using publicly available information.

Mandelker (1974)

Mergers are generally anticipated in efficient capital markets. In the USA, Mandelker found that shareholders began to anticipate mergers about eight months before the event.

Strong form tests of the EMH

Friend, Brown, Herman and Vickers (1962)

This was a pioneering study of the performance of 189 US mutual funds (unit trusts) for the period 1952–8. The fundamental conclusion of the study was that the funds, on average, performed no better and no worse than the composite markets from which they selected securities. Although some funds performed better than others over the $5\frac{3}{4}$ years studied, there was little evidence of a consistent tendency towards superior or inferior performance on a year-to-year basis by individual funds. Furthermore, although some funds were far more active than others, there was no consistent relationship between portfolio turnover and portfolio performance for either the current year or the following year.

Sharpe (1966)

Sharpe studied the performance of 34 US mutual funds during the period 1954–63. He found that the linear relationship predicted by the capital asset pricing model appeared to hold. Funds with large average returns typically showed greater variability than those with smaller average returns. However, there were differences in efficiency, and there appeared to be some tendency for the level of efficiency to persist. Funds with low rankings during the period 1944–53 tended to have low rankings during the later period, 1954–63. Good performance was found to be associated with a low level of expenses. Fund size was found to be an unimportant predictor of performance. Only 11 of the funds outperformed the Dow-Jones Average, while 23 underperformed. The study generally supports the view that capital markets are efficient, and that good portfolio managers concentrate on evaluating risk, providing diversification, and spending a small proportion of the fund on searching out underpriced securities.

Jensen (1968)

This is a study of 115 US mutual funds for the period 1945–64. Using a CAPM approach to portfolio performance measurement, Jensen attempted to find positive risk-adjusted excess returns (α^*s), which would suggest superior performance. A naïve selection buy-and-hold policy can be expected to yield an α^* of zero. Poor performance should result in a negative α^*. On average, funds earned about 1.1 per cent less per annum than would have been expected given their levels of systematic risk (beta). They were, therefore, on average, not able to predict security prices well enough to outperform a buy-the-market-and-hold strategy. Furthermore, on average, the funds were not sufficiently successful in their trading activity to recoup even their brokerage expenses, let alone their research and administration costs. Finally, successful past performance could not be used as a predictor of future success. Jensen's findings are therefore consistent with the efficient market hypothesis.

Friend, Blume and Crockett (1970)

These authors studied the performance of 136 mutual funds for the period 1960–8. They found that the funds had not generally matched the performance of equally distributed random investments in the New York Stock Exchange, but that they had fully matched the performance of proportionally distributed random investments in NYSE stock. High-risk funds had actually surpassed such random performance, especially during the period 1964–8. When the funds were classified by fund size, sales charges, management expenses, portfolio turnover, and investment objectives, no consistent relationship was found between these factors and investment performance when the latter was adjusted for risk. As in previous studies, the evidence generally supports the strong form of the EMH in that there is little evidence of stock market professionals being able consistently to achieve returns which more than compensate for market risk.

Firth (1978)

In the UK, Firth has studied the performance of 360 unit trusts for the period 1967–75. Conclusions generally support the American findings. Unit trust performance conforms closely to expected performance based on the CAPM. The positive and negative α^*s are so small that the general conclusion is that the unit trust industry's investment performance matches the market, after adjusting for risk. As α^*s showed very low stability from one period to the next, the implication is that past performance gives no guide to future performance. It appears that in the UK unit trust managers do not have access to non-public information or skills which enable them to achieve abnormal returns.

Stock market inefficiency

Niederhoffer and Osborne (1966)

Some inefficiency in the weak form of the EMH was indicated earlier, in the Niederhoffer and Osborne study of 1966. To some extent, prices appear to ebb and flow during the course of the day, suggesting some slight pattern. This is very mild evidence against the weak form of the EMH. The more serious result of their study relates to insider trading. It does appear that the specialist on the New York Stock Exchange (the closest comparable function in the UK is that of the market maker), who has access to advance notice of buy and sell transactions (limit orders), can consistently achieve superior returns. In fact, specialists earn a positive excess return on the vast majority of their own transactions. This is evidence against the strong form of the efficient market hypothesis, since share prices do not apparently reflect *all* information, including that which is not public. Specialists can use non-public information to earn excess returns. This comes as little surprise to anybody. We should expect (and we have all heard tales to the effect) that an insider having price-sensitive information can make abnormal profits.

Scholes (1972)

The Scholes study of 1972, already referred to, also suggests that corporate insiders have access to price-sensitive information. Large block disposals by corporations and officers of corporations are associated with the greatest price declines. Corporate officers might use this information to make profits. Again, we should not be surprised at the existence of inside information. We are not surprised that it can be used to earn abnormal returns. For the recipient of inside information, there are legal pitfalls to be considered before making use of such information.

Jaffe (1974)

The 1974 study of inside information by Jaffe confirms that insiders earn abnormal returns. Clearly, the strong form of the EMH does not hold absolutely. A second finding of the study is that in the USA the laws against insider trading have very little effect in stopping it!

Ambachtsheer (1974)

Perhaps the best news for portfolio managers comes from studies similar to that of Ambachtsheer in 1974. Apparently, some investors do have the ability to forecast specific returns. Such forecasting ability has not been obvious from the many studies of unit trust performance. In the absence of forecasting ability, we should expect studies to find a zero correlation between forecast and actual outcomes. However, Ambachtsheer found a correlation of 0.16. Even low forecasting ability, such as this represents, is useful in achieving abnormal returns but, unfortunately, forecasting ability is very hard to find. Discovering it requires the comparison of many forecasts with actual results, as the forecaster could have a lucky run.

Dimson and Marsh (1984)

In one of the largest studies in the UK, these authors examined the ability of analysts to forecast annual returns on over 200 of the largest shares quoted on the UK market. They found that the correlation between forecast returns and actual returns amounted to a modest 0.08. Nonetheless, actual transactions which were carried out after the forecasts outperformed the market by 2.2 per cent in the year following the trade, and this represented an abnormal return of £3.0 million. However, Dimson and Marsh also found that over half the informational content of the forecasts was reflected in stock prices by the end of the first month after the forecast. Any favoured client of the broker who received a recommendation based on the forecast would have had to act quickly to benefit from the advice. The results of this research mirror closely those of Ambachtsheer which were described above.

Conclusion

A vast quantity of research evidence supports the EMH in the weak form, the semi-strong form, and the strong form. We have briefly summarized a few studies. There is evidence of market inefficiency, particularly in the case of the strong form of the EMH, and excess returns can be made with luck, inside information and, the best news so far, forecasting ability.

Further reading

Copeland, T. E., and J. F. Weston: *Financial Theory and Corporate Policy*, London, Addison-Wesley, 1988, chapters 10 and 11.

Dyckman, T. R., D. H. Downes and R. P. Magee: *Efficient Capital Markets and Accounting: A Critical Analysis*, Hemel Hempstead, Prentice-Hall, 1975.

Elton, E. J., and M. J. Gruber: *Modern Portfolio Theory and Investment Analysis*, 4th edn, New York, John Wiley, 1991, chapter 15.

Fama, E. F.: Efficient Capital Markets: A Review of Theory and Empirical Work. *Journal of Finance*, 25, May 1970, pp. 383–417.

5

Implications of the efficient market hypothesis

Introduction

The efficient market hypothesis (EMH) asserts that share prices fully reflect all available information, any new or shock information being very rapidly incorporated into the share price. This apparently simple hypothesis, if true, has very powerful implications for investment analysis and corporate management. A great deal of evidence reported in chapter 4 supports the hypothesis. For the vast majority of investors, with little or no inside information, unproven forecasting ability, and no expectation of consistently good luck, stock markets are highly competitive, very efficient markets. It appears that modern stock markets are efficient in that share prices tend to reflect all available information.

At first glance, the EMH is readily acceptable to students, managers and even stock market professionals. Surely, in very competitive, open markets such as the New York, American and London stock exchanges, the activities of millions of market participants will generate the equilibrium price which reflects expectations about cash flows and market risk. Surely, in these competitive markets we would expect share prices to react immediately to new information affecting anticipations. The hypothesis of efficient capital markets seems reasonable and fairly harmless – until we examine its implications. Once we discuss the implications of the EMH, many students, managers and particularly stock market professionals become strongly opposed to the idea of market efficiency. A great deal of argument has taken place over the last 30 years relating to the level of stock market efficiency. This chapter lists the implications of the EMH. It should be obvious to the reader why the suggestion of market efficiency has been so unpopular, particularly with the professional investment community.

Implications for individual security selection

Technical analysis (chartism)

The basic premise of technical analysis is that past share prices and data relating to past trading activity can be used to predict future prices. A vast quantity of weak form testing of the EMH suggests that past movements cannot be used to predict future movements. The study of past share price movements cannot help the investor to achieve excess returns. Historic data are publicly available information, and any implications of history for the future are, therefore, already incorporated into the current share price. Of course, examination of the movement of share prices might suggest, with hindsight, that the share price was following a trend. However, even completely random share price movements plotted over time can appear to have followed a pattern or trend. This does not mean that the price was actually following a predictable trend. The share price did not know where it had been, and did not know where it was going. We would expect some techniques to appear to work over certain restricted time-periods. The EMH implies that the net present value of any security acquisition is zero – that is, investors pay the market price for investments. Market prices are the best estimates of present value.

We should always add a humble note on our dismissal of technical analysis – it could just be that some little old lady in Bournemouth has worked out all the cycles and patterns and is laughing all the way to the bank. She is quite right to keep it quiet. For the professional chartists, the onus is on them to prove that they consistently make excess returns.

Fundamental analysis

Fundamental or intrinsic value analysts try to estimate the 'real' value of securities, as opposed to the market value. They assume that the market has probably got it wrong. The EMH suggests that the best estimate of a company's value is the current market value, which is generated by the trading activity of large numbers of wealth maximizers buying and selling shares with real money in highly competitive markets. Investors make their decisions in the light of all available information. New or shock information is rapidly incorporated into the share price together with all other information. It is therefore not necessary for the individual to take a view as to the appropriateness of the current share price. An investor can accept the existing market price as the best estimate of intrinsic or 'real' value. The fact that a great many professional investors with vast data banks, highly skilled investment analysts and computer departments are very busy trying to beat the market is very comforting for the individual investor, who can accept the generated market price as the consensus view. It is not necessary for individuals to try to predict a firm's cash flows for the next 25 years and discount those cash flows at some required rate of return to arrive at the fundamental or intrinsic value. Highly competitive securities markets price assets efficiently.

— Semi-Strong (handwritten annotation)

Bargain hunting

There are no bargains in efficient capital markets. On occasion, of course, an investor with luck, inside information, or forecasting ability can achieve superior performance, but in competitive markets the risky cash flows attaching to individual securities are extremely interchangeable. Equity markets are very active, particularly for the unit trust sector, and in such active and competitive markets, we should not expect to find any bargains. The net present value of any acquisition should be zero.

The value of tipsters

When share prices fully reflect all available information, then individual newspaper tipsters, bank managers, accountants and stockbrokers should not be expected to recommend consistently those shares which will outperform other shares of similar risk. We should only expect a tip to be of value when the tipster has persistent luck, forecasting ability or inside information (and knows how the market will react when the information becomes public). We are aware of the reputations attaching to some eminent share price forecasters. For those who want to believe in the forecasting business, we suggest that even in efficient random walk markets, if you predict a share price will go up, you will get it right about 50 per cent of the time – think about it! Whether the tipster recommends specific securities or market movements, the onus is on the tipster to demonstrate continuous successful performance.

The study of published accounts

A whole lifetime can be spent by investors studying the wealth of accounting data and press coverage relating to companies, industries and economies. For the individual investor or portfolio manager, such study is almost certainly a waste of time, as all such available information is already reflected in the share price. If the investor can demonstrate consistently that excess returns are achieved by the use of in-depth analysis of publicly available information, then he can undermine the validity of the EMH by demonstrating forecasting ability. Forecasting ability is rather difficult to prove, and although there is some evidence that some investors do have forecasting ability, the discovery of the achievement of excess returns has generally eluded researchers except where the investor has access to inside information.

Accounting policies

Investors are not fooled by accounting policies relating to stock valuation, depreciation, debtors and accrued income, creditors and accrued expenses, or treatment of research and development. A sufficient number of investors understand the difference between profit flow and cash flow: a change in stock valuation policies will affect reported profit but not cash flow; depreciation charges reduce reported profit but do not affect cash flow. Development expenditure may be capitalized and appear in the balance sheet as an asset, but efficient markets realize that such payments reduce cash flow. An increased investment in stock and debtors may not affect reported profit, but such additional investment must be financed using cash. Capital investment requires cash financing, but the amount of the investment will probably be written off as an expense in the profit and loss account over the asset's estimated useful life. Shareholders are apparently not fooled by accounting policies or changes in accounting policies. They capitalize expected cash flows.

Accountants may not welcome a theory of competitive markets which suggests that shareholders can see through the veil of financial accounting. They may believe their status is threatened. As we observe the high rate of activity in the generation of financial accounting standards around the world, it would be comforting to assume that shareholders accept such accounting documents at face value and even to assume that reported levels of profits, assets and sales determine share prices. Efficient stock markets, however, are apparently not fooled by accounting policies. Competitive market participants make unbiased estimates of future cash flows and discount them at a rate which reflects market risk, thereby determining the present value of securities.

Value of more accounting disclosure

Published (audited) accounts never seem to get any shorter. However, in efficient markets, historic movements in share prices and knowledge of historic accounting data are of no value to investors in their attempts to predict the direction of future share price movements. This does not mean that improved accounting standards or additional disclosures are useless. It simply means that since investors are likely to have equal access to this information, it gives no single investor an advantage over the others. Investors seem to have little difficulty in seeing through accounting manipulations. All available information relating to future cash flows is already reflected in the share price, including any possibility of forecasting future cash flows from historic cash flows. Investors are not fooled by accounts unadjusted for inflation; they have heard of it and take it into account in generating market prices. Tax gatherers, wage bargainers, lenders, and even company directors in their generous dividend payments, may be fooled – but not investors in efficient markets. It therefore appears that the wealth of historic accounting and legal data contained in published accounts need not be increased for shareholders to take a rational view of a firm's investment schedule. Even information relating to the future is only of value in changing a company's share price if that information has not already been anticipated by investors. Furthermore, as already stated, investors are not likely to be fooled by changes in accounting policies relating to depreciation, research and development or revaluation of assets. Neither are they fooled by the issue of bonus shares. A share purchaser buys a stake in the firm's future operational cash flows. Investors are not fooled by the document giving title to that cash flow stake; a 10 per cent stake consisting of 1,000 shares is worth the same as a 10 per cent stake consisting of 1,500 shares.

Of course, there may be other reasons why companies should disclose information, relating to employment, customer services, balance of payments, taxation, and environmental and other social factors. It may also be of value to produce inflation-adjusted statements for the guidance of the Treasury, wage bargainers, banks and formulators of dividend policies. Information which would be of interest to shareholders is shock information which would change their forecasts of cash flow and risk.

Share price reaction to new information

In an efficient market, share prices reflect expectations. Investors take a view about future net operational cash flow and risk. Therefore, when a company's earnings for the current year are announced as being a significant improvement on the preceding year, we should not expect the share price either to rise or fall. On average, the market gets it right. Only the shock announcements result in price changes, and share prices do change very rapidly on the announcement of new information relating to expected cash flow and risk. Economic information contained in the announcement of a stock split is anticipated, no excess returns being achieved following the announcement; and if the stock split does not contain economic information, then we would not expect the share price to move at all. Large secondary offerings and block sales of securities result in price declines when the issuer is a corporation or corporate officer, suggesting that the offer implies bad news and that the market reacts quickly and in an unbiased manner to such information. However, if the offer is by an individual, bank, insurance company or trustee, then the security price does not decline significantly, suggesting that such a sale does not imply bad news. In so far as earnings announcements and dividend announcements affect expectations, either they are anticipated or the new shock information is rapidly incorporated into the share price. In efficient markets, only shock information results in price movements.

Significance of a single security

In efficient markets, share prices reflect expectations. Prices reflect anticipated returns and perceived risk, the net present value of all investments and portfolios is zero, and investors pay the market price for securities and portfolios. The overriding implication of modern portfolio theory is that an individual security should be assessed in terms of its contribution to the expected return and riskiness of the portfolio. Diversification can remove the specific risk associated with an individual security so that its contribution to the risk of the portfolio is its market risk. Market risk can be measured by beta, and the beta of a portfolio is the weighted average of all the betas associated with individual securities. The riskiness of an individual security is of importance in so far as it affects the overall beta of the portfolio.

Implications for portfolio management

Modern portfolio theory and investor behaviour

One of the attractive features of modern portfolio theory is that it explains the way in which many people have always behaved. MPT assumes investor rationality. Investors have traditionally invested in a mixture of government securities (a proxy for the risk-free rate of interest) and unit trusts or a selection of equities (a proxy for the market portfolio). Seekers of high-risk investments can borrow money to play the stock market. The CML explains this rational behaviour. Modern portfolio theory enables investors to identify high-risk and low-risk portfolios and to expect portfolio returns commensurate with the level of accepted market risk as indicated by the CAPM.

At the same time, we should mention that one of the numerous criticisms of the EMH is that many investors do not diversify efficiently. They do not behave in a manner which suggests that they accept the EMH. In particular, many investors try to identify underpriced stocks. This behaviour does not mean that stock markets are inefficient. In fact, it is the highly competitive activity of investors which makes the market efficient. For the market to be efficient, it is necessary that many people do not believe that it is efficient. This highly competitive behaviour leads us to conclude that the only way that investors can make excess returns is by luck, by access to inside information, or by proven forecasting ability.

Investment counselling

Investment advisers with some sympathy for the efficient market hypothesis will cease to offer clients a series of tips and a very high level of portfolio activity. They might consider the following actions:

1 Present the investor with the CAPM and explain its importance.
2 Establish the investor's risk–return preference (that is, the preferred point along the security market line).
3 Diversify away unsystematic risk, for which there are no rewards, by finding a surrogate for the market portfolio, such as a well-diversified unit trust, or an index fund.
4 Consider and advise on income tax and capital gains tax.
5 Avoid transaction costs.
6 Conduct a regular review of the portfolio to maintain the investor's preferred position on the security market line.

Mechanical methods for making money

There are no mechanical systems for making excess returns. As we have seen from the last chapter, many of these systems have been exhaustively tested and no systematic method of making excess returns has been found. Consistent above-average returns have not generally been associated with individual professional managers, other than those having access to inside information – corporate insiders and specialists. Recent evidence does suggest that it is possible for skilled professionals to have some forecasting ability. Modern portfolio theory provides a mechanical framework for making portfolio decisions by presenting the investor with the security market line and allowing the investor to choose a defensive or aggressive porfolio. A defensive portfolio may consist of a mixture of risk-free securities and the market portfolio. An aggressive portfolio can be achieved by borrowing money and investing in the market portfolio. The investor may wish to take a view with regard to market movements and choose a high-beta portfolio in an anticipated bull market or a low-beta portfolio in an anticipated bear market. In an anticipated bear market the investor can also 'go liquid'. An investor who feels he or she has special skills in predicting a company's specific successes and failures which are not related to general market movements can focus attention on companies with high levels of specific risk.

Institutional investors

Many people have heard the rumour that stock market prices are determined by a few people in the know. These powerful financiers apparently have the muscle to peg prices or push them up and down at will. There is a great deal of evidence which suggests that this is not true. Large block transactions do not result in volatile price movements, unless the market feels that the transactions convey economic information attributable to the inside knowledge of the trader. As has been witnessed on many occasions in foreign exchange markets, it requires a great deal of money to push prices to where the market does not think prices ought to be.

Dollar averaging

Many pamphlets and even text books recommend the dollar averaging technique for making money. It goes like this. You have £1,000 per period to invest, and buy 1,000 shares in a company (or units in a unit trust) at £1 each. The share price falls to 50p, but you continue to invest £1,000 per period in the same stock. You now get 2,000 shares for your £1,000 and the average cost falls to 67p, 3,000 shares for £2,000. This makes you feel warm all over (you completely ignore the fact that you have lost £500 on the first investment). As the company's share price continues its decline, you get more and more shares for your periodic £1,000, and the average cost of purchasing falls with each additional acquisition. Eventually, the company goes into liquidation and you lose all your money. Your consolation is that because you had many thousands of shares, your average loss per share is very small indeed!

Efficient stock markets reward unavoidable risk-taking

In efficient markets there are no rewards for taking on risks which can be avoided, and investors can avoid specific risk by diversification. Rewards are offered only for market risk, which cannot be avoided. The measure of market risk is beta, and we should therefore expect a linear trade-off between expected return and beta, as illustrated by the CAPM. For the majority of investors, it seems sensible to diversify away specific risk and construct a defensive or aggressive portfolio of the required market risk.

Portfolio diversification

Non-market, diversifiable, avoidable or specific risk can be removed by diversification; that is, diversification removes the specific risk relating to individual securities. Diversification does not remove the market risk, which is related to general movements in anticipations about the economy, but investors with diversified portfolios need not worry about the shock disappointments of individual companies, as these are balanced out by shock successes of other companies in the portfolio. Investment in 50 to 60 securities removes a high proportion of non-market risk. This diversifiable risk can be removed completely by investment in the market portfolio, which is a weighted investment in all securities. A highly diversified unit trust is a reasonable surrogate for the market portfolio.

Non-systematic risk can be avoided by diversification. Therefore, in an efficient market there are no rewards for accepting diversifiable risk, but rewards exist for acceptance of market risk. (Local market risk can, to some extent, be avoided by international diversification.) Investors can take a view as to the direction of the market and invest in high-beta securities in anticipated bull markets and low-beta securities in anticipated bear markets. Alternatively, investors can hold low-beta portfolios by investing in a mixture of government securities and equities, and can invest in portfolios with betas greater than 1 by borrowing and investing in the market portfolio. In figure 5.1, portfolio A is a low-risk portfolio with $\beta < 1$. B is a portfolio with systematic risk equal to that of the market portfolio ($\beta = 1$). C is a high-risk portfolio with $\beta > 1$. The line $R_F C$ is the security market line, R_F being the risk-free rate of interest and R_M being the return of the market portfolio. The market portfolio has a beta of 1, since it obviously moves in perfect lockstep with itself.

Unit trust performance

Unit trust advertisements generally promise diversification and suggest some likely 'performance'. A great many studies show that

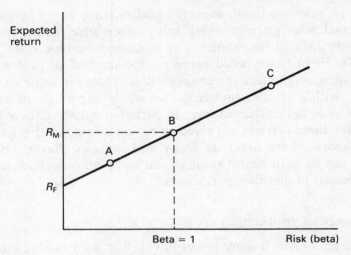

Figure 5.1 Portfolio selection

unit trusts offer diversification but not performance. Returns are generally in line with expected returns given the portfolio beta. The offer of diversification by unit trusts is a useful service, as they provide extreme diversification at very low cost for investors of modest as well as immodest means. Performance claims should be viewed with caution. The other worrying aspect of unit trust management is the trusts' very high level of market activity, which incurs heavy transaction costs. In addition, trusts frequently diversify into risk-free securities and this results in portfolios with very low betas.

Unit trust performance tables appearing in the popular press and television programmes should also be viewed with caution. Even now, many league tables ignore risk completely. The 'winner' in a recent British TV unit trust competition turned out to be a trust dominated by gold, but, fortunately, the manager of the 'winning' trust was quick to point out that the trust is very high-risk and completely unsuitable for widows and orphans. We would clearly expect high-risk unit trusts to perform well *vis à vis* the market in some years, and equally badly in other years.

Measurement of portfolio performance

If we accept modern portfolio theory, then the expected return of a portfolio is a function of the portfolio beta. Actual performance should be compared with expected performance based perhaps on the capital asset pricing model, but performance measurement is extremely difficult (in chapter 3 we discussed the objections to the CAPM). Even if we could agree on the method of performance appraisal, we could face the phenomenon of luck. In a game of pure chance, with no transaction costs, we would expect about half the players to do better than average in period one, half of these would do better than average in period two, and so on. In this game of pure chance, there are only lucky and unlucky players, but we should not be surprised if some of the lucky players claim to have skills denied to all other participants.

Avoidance of transaction costs

In a market in which share prices fully reflect all available information, and in which the net present value of all acquisitions is zero, there is little point in continuous switching from one security to another. Switching investments incurs transaction costs and the possibility of taxation. Modern portfolio theory suggests that investors should choose their preferred portfolio and then avoid transaction costs by pursuing buy-and-hold policies, revising the portfolio on occasion to maintain the preferred level of risk.

Passive management

Those investors who accept the EMH should not devote their time and financial resources to active management, seeking out under-priced securities. One low-cost strategy is to identify the required level of market risk and use an index fund which satisfies the investor's requirement. Alternatively, a well-diversified unit trust can be linked to a level of borrowing or lending. The cost of pension fund portfolio management can be very low if a fund's trustees use a professional service offering the required level of risk, rather than employing investment analysts with their associated office, information, and computing costs.

Active–passive management

Those who are almost, but not completely, convinced by the arguments supporting the EMH can adopt active–passive portfolio management. Perhaps 80 per cent of a fund can be passively managed by indexation, and the remaining 20 per cent can be actively managed, particularly where:

1 an investor or fund manager feels he or she has investment expertise in forecasting returns on individual securities;
2 the manager has expertise in forecasting market movements;
3 the manager has inside information (and is familiar with the legal requirements for its use); and
4 an investor is prepared to try his or her luck.

The performance of the actively managed portion of the total portfolio can be measured on a regular basis, taking into account its riskiness and the costs of management.

Implications for financial management

Corporate objectives

The primary objective of industrial organizations is to create wealth. This is achieved when the market value of the outputs (cash inflow) is greater than the market value of the inputs (cash outflow), taking into account the timing and risk of the firm's cash flows. Industrial projects, products, and mergers (investment decisions) should be taken on when they offer positive net present values. When a firm takes on a wealth-creating project, its market value is increased when such information is reflected in share prices, and we can therefore suggest that the primary objective of industrial organizations is the maximization of the present value of the firm's securities. Even when firms consider environmental and social issues, they should still consider the effect of their investment and financing decisions on the value of the firm's securities.

The trade-off between risk and return

In efficient capital markets there is a linear trade-off between risk and return along the lines suggested by the CAPM. Investors expect higher returns for accepting greater risk. Borrowing from the bank at 12 per cent and investing in equities expected to earn 20 per cent sounds like a good idea, but the investor has a very high risk of considerable loss, should equity prices fall. Putting cash into a deposit account for one year will earn only a few percentage points, but there is a very high probability of actually collecting. We postulate a positive linear relationship between risk and expected return.

In figure 5.2, investment A is risk-free – that is, an investment in Treasury bills, or a deposit with a building society or bank – and investment B is a high-risk, high-return project. If an investor must choose between investment A or B (which of course he need not do), then his decision will depend on his willingness to accept increasing risk for an increased expected return. Some people really do undertake very risky investments and others really do undertake risk-free investments, and some people do both. Assuming A and B are the only two available investments, the investment opportunities for investors who diversify lie along the line AB. The position their investments occupy along this line will depend on the proportion of their funds invested in each security.

Suppose now that instead of considering investments on the stock market, we are acting as managers of a firm trying to maximize shareholder wealth. On the introduction of projects C to H, we must always prefer D to C because it offers the same expected return for a lower risk. For the same reason, E is always preferable to F. C is preferred to F as it offers a higher expected return for the same risk, and for the same reason D is preferred to E. In fact, as rational wealth maximizers, we are continually trying to reach project H, the investment which offers very high expected returns for very low risk. The problem with project H is that it is difficult to

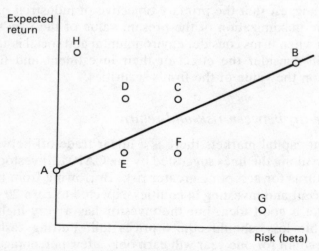

Figure 5.2   Trade-off between risk and return

find. However, in order to maximize the market value of the firm, managers should continually seek out projects above the line AB – that is, projects with positive net present values, the acceptance of which increases the market value of the firm. In product markets, the finding of such projects is difficult but possible. In highly competitive, very active stock markets, it does appear to be extremely difficult consistently to achieve rewards above those expected for the level of market risk accepted. In efficient capital markets, the line AB is the security market line and the demand for investment H would be immediately so great that its price would rise and therefore its expected return fall vertically onto the line AB. Investment G is a high-risk, low-return project. In product markets, managers will avoid it. In competitive capital markets, its price would fall, thereby pushing up its expected return vertically onto the line AB. The competitive activity of many buyers and sellers pushes all projects, including projects C to H, towards the line AB.

Capital budgeting

The linear trade-off between risk and expected return can help to identify the required rates of return on industrial and commercial projects. To plot the security market line it is necessary to identify the risk-free rate of interest and the return on the market portfolio. The market portfolio has a beta coefficient of 1. The firm's beta can be calculated by regressing its periodic returns on the periodic returns of the market index, or, alternatively, it may be located in the quarterly *Risk Measurement Service* publication issued by the London Business School. The firm's beta identifies the average required rate of return from the security market line. However, this average cost of capital (required rate of return) cannot be used for individual projects. There is a trade-off between risk and expected return, and it is theoretically necessary to estimate a beta coefficient for each individual project within the firm. This is impossible at the present time, but all that is necessary for practical purposes is for projects to be classified into, say, three or five risk categories, as illustrated in figure 5.3.

Assuming the historic risk-free rate of interest to be 6 per cent and the average historic risk premium for investment in the market portfolio to be 9 per cent, then a firm with a beta of unity might classify its projects into three groups – low-risk A, average-risk B and high-risk C. Required rates of return might be 6 per cent to

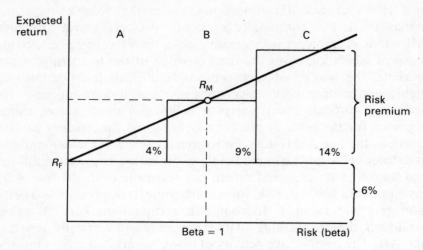

Figure 5.3   Classification of projects into risk categories

cover the risk-free rate of interest plus risk premia of 4 per cent, 9 per cent and 14 per cent, giving required rates of return of 10 per cent for group A, 15 per cent for group B, and 20 per cent for group C. The procedure is obviously crude, but it is an improvement on payback, return on book value, and net present value using the estimated overall cost of capital (required rate of return) regardless of the riskiness of individual projects. For divisionalized companies, rates of return can be generated for each division by identifying the betas of independent quoted companies in the same business or risk class. As a cautionary note, we should add that betas are influenced by economic risk and financial risk. Financial risk arises on the introduction of debt into a firm's capital structure. Projects should offer returns commensurate with their economic risk, and it is therefore necessary to reduce the reported corporate beta to an unlevered corporate beta for the purposes of capital expenditure analysis.

Company valuation

When asked to calculate the value of a listed company, it is not necessary to study balance sheets, profit and loss accounts, statements of sources and applications of funds, chairmen's reports, price–earnings ratios, and dividend and earnings yields. The best estimate of the value of the company's equity is its market capitalization. That is the price of each of its shares multiplied by the number of shares in issue. Market capitalization is published daily, except Mondays, in the *Financial Times*. To compute the total value of the company, the market value of its debt is added to the market value of its equity. Unquoted company valuation should be based on anticipated net operational cash flows discounted at the rate of return relating to a quoted company in the same risk class or industry. For unquoted company valuation, analysts can measure the volatility of historic company cash flows or reported earnings against the volatility of the industry cash flows or earnings to generate crude estimates of beta based on accounting numbers.

Mergers and takeovers

In an efficient market the buyer pays a fair price. He is unlikely to be able to search out and find any undervalued companies. This, of course, does not mean that there are no profitable or unprofitable acquisitions. The new management may bring skills to the acquired company and may be able to revitalize its fortunes. It may be able to cut costs, improve efficiency and alter the strategy of the acquired company. However, these gains are likely to arise from the skills of the acquirer in managing the acquisition, rather than from a bargain purchase. In a similar manner, the acquirer may fail to bring to the acquired company the necessary skills for its development, and the acquisition may turn out to be a failure.

For any bid to succeed, a premium must be paid over the pre-bid price of the company. Usually this is a minimum 10 per cent, and it is not unknown for the premium to exceed 60 per cent. Often the pre-bid price will reflect the possibility of a merger, since there may well have been speculation of an impending bid in the press. The shareholders in the acquired firm nearly always make an immediate gain. What is less certain is whether the buyer profits. If a large premium is paid, the buyer will have to work very hard or bring very special skills to the acquisition to recoup the premium. In a competitive market place it is likely that there will be competition amongst predators for poorly managed companies. If the market is perfectly competitive, then gains will all go to the acquired firm's shareholders, leaving no special gains for the acquirer's shareholders.

Corporate diversification

Why do boards of directors try to turn public companies into unit trusts? Survival of top management is a powerful managerial motivation and the probability of survival can be increased by corporate diversification. It is not necessary for companies to provide diversification for shareholders, as investors can and do diversify their holdings across a number of companies. Shareholders often object to corporate diversification on the grounds that they can achieve such diversification without the aid of management, but corporate diversification does achieve employment diversification for management and employees. Conglomerate diversification (where there is no synergy and where there are no economies of scale) in fact reduces investor choice by removing individual companies from the market place.

In addition, there are strong arguments which suggest that it is best for companies to devote their energies to areas in which they have a distinctive competence or competitive advantage. Diversification may lead them to technologies or markets which they fail to understand fully. The break-ups of many conglomerates, such as Imperial Tobacco or BAT, provide recent examples where directors have decided that value can be added by de-mergers.

Dividend policy

The traditional view in investment management is that the purchaser of a share buys a dividend expectation and that dividends are worth more to investors than retained earnings. Again, if we accept that the market value of the firm is based on the anticipated net operational cash flows from the firm's investment schedule, then a company which is expected to generate £6,000 per annum in an industry which capitalizes those cash flows at 20 per cent will be valued at £30,000:

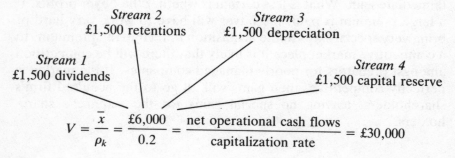

$$V = \frac{\bar{x}}{\rho_k} = \frac{£6,000}{0.2} = \frac{\text{net operational cash flows}}{\text{capitalization rate}} = £30,000$$

The net operational cash flows may be called dividends, retentions, depreciation, transfer to capital reserve, revenue reserve, plant replacement reserve, or deferred taxation. Do we accept the present value formula or is it necessary to value the different streams into which the cash flows are divided by devising weighting factors for each stream? Modern portfolio theory suggests that we accept the present value formula, the dividend decision, given the firm's investment decision, being irrelevant to shareholder returns (ignoring taxation and transaction costs).

The mathematical proof of dividend irrelevance is summarized below.

The one-period expected returns of securities of all firms in a given risk class must be the same in any given period, otherwise investors would hold only the securities with the highest return, and this would be inconsistent with equilibrium in the sense of market clearing. So for any period t, and for all firms in a given risk class, we have

$$r_{t+1} = \frac{d_{t+1} + v_{t+1} - v_t}{v_t} \tag{5.1}$$

where r is the rate of return appropriate to the risk class, d is the dividend per share, and v is the price per share.

Rewriting equation (5.1) gives

$$v_t r_{t+1} + v_t = d_{t+1} + v_{t+1}.$$

Therefore

$$v_t = \frac{1}{1 + r_{t+1}} (d_{t+1} + v_{t+1}). \tag{5.2}$$

Equation (5.2) shows the present value of a share. In order to obtain the total value of all the firm's shares, that is, the current value of the firm, we simply multiply by n, the number of shares, giving

$$n_t v_t = \frac{1}{1 + r_{t+1}} (n_t d_{t+1} + n_t v_{t+1}).$$

Therefore

$$V_t = \frac{1}{1 + r_{t+1}} (D_{t+1} + n_t v_{t+1}) \tag{5.3}$$

where $V_t = n_t v_t$ is the value of the firm, and $D_{t+1} = n_t d_{t+1}$ represents the total dividends paid by the firm.

If m new shares are issued at time $t + 1$ at the then ruling price v_{t+1}, then

$$V_{t+1} = n_{t+1}v_{t+1}$$
$$= n_t v_{t+1} + m_{t+1}v_{t+1}.$$

Hence

$$n_t v_{t+1} = V_{t+1} - m_{t+1}v_{t+1}. \tag{5.4}$$

Substituting equation (5.4) into equation (5.3) gives

$$V_t = \frac{1}{1 + r_{t+1}} (D_{t+1} + V_{t+1} - m_{t+1}v_{t+1}). \tag{5.5}$$

That is, the value of shares existing at time t is equal to the present value of the dividend payable at time $t + 1$, plus the present value of all shares existing at time $t + 1$, minus the present value of new shares issued at time $t + 1$.

Now, as finance people, we all know that sources of funds always equal applications of funds, so

$$R_{t+1} + m_{t+1}v_{t+1} = D_{t+1} + W_{t+1} + I_{t+1} \tag{5.6}$$

where R is operating receipts, W is wages and other operating expenses, and I is capital investment.

Rearranging equation (5.6) gives

$$-m_{t+1}v_{t+1} = R_{t+1} - D_{t+1} - W_{t+1} - I_{t+1}. \tag{5.7}$$

Substituting equation (5.7) into equation (5.5) yields

$$V_t = \frac{1}{1 + r_{t+1}} (R_{t+1} - W_{t+1} - I_{t+1} + V_{t+1}). \tag{5.8}$$

As D_{t+1} does not appear in equation (5.8), the value of the firm is completely independent of its dividend policy. The present valuation depends on the required rate of return appropriate to the risk class of the firm over the next time-period, the firm's operating income and investment outlays over the next time-period, and the market value of the company's shares at the end of the next time-period. However, this latter factor, V_{t+1}, simply depends upon future required rates of return, operating incomes and investment outlays. From equation (5.8) we get

$$V_{t+1} = \frac{1}{1 + r_{t+2}} (R_{t+2} - W_{t+2} - I_{t+2} + V_{t+2}).$$

Given a firm's operating policies, the particular dividend policy adopted has no effect on the current market value of the firm. The value of the firm depends on its investment schedule. Given efficient capital markets, and ignoring transaction costs and taxation, an increase in the dividend reduces the investment schedule, and, therefore, reduces the ex-dividend price of the equity by the same amount. It is the investment policy, not the financing arrangements, which determines the value of the enterprise. A change in dividend policy implies a change in the distribution of total returns between dividends and capital gains.

When we desert the world of mathematical proof and return to the world of taxation, transaction costs and information content of dividends, the role of dividend policy in firm valuation becomes more complex. Historically, high rates of personal taxation have favoured retentions. Furthermore, transaction costs discourage companies from making generous dividend payments when they have surplus cash and making rights issues when profitable investment opportunities arise at a later time. Some institutions which are tax-exempt, for example pension funds, may be indifferent between dividends and capital gains. Currently, the highest rate of income tax, at 40 per cent, is, by historical standards, low. Furthermore, subject to an annual exemption for the first £5,800 of gains, capital gains are taxed in the same way as income – that is, at the highest marginal rate of the tax-payer. Tax is now a less important issue than it used to be for the formulation dividend policy. Historically, some firms in the growth phase of their life cycle paid out low dividends. The shares of these companies appealed to wealthy individuals whose incomes were taxed at very high rates. Such companies probably tended to attract a clientele of wealthy individuals as shareholders. Conversely, companies which paid out generous dividends perhaps tended to gather a following among less wealthy individuals who paid lower marginal rates of income tax. Clearly when companies enter a new phase of their development and change their dividend policy, it is sensible for them to do this gradually.

A surprise increase in dividends is often accompanied by increases in share prices, and vice versa. How can this be, in a world where dividend policy has been shown to be irrelevant? The answer is simple. At times when dividend changes are announced, other information about the firm's future prospects is also released. A surprise increase in dividends is generally taken as a compelling signal that the directors have confidence in the future prosperity of the firm. In other words, it is not the paying of cash from one pocket, the company's, to another, the shareholders', which creates wealth, but the good news which accompanies this payment.

Capital structure

The market value of a firm is its discounted net anticipated operational cash flows:

$$V = S_{mv} + D_{mv} = \sum_{t=1}^{n} \frac{1}{(1 + r)^t} (OR - OE - I)_t$$

$$= \frac{\bar{x}}{\rho_k} = \sum_{t=1}^{n} \frac{R_t}{(1 + r)^t}$$

where

t = time-period, 1, . . ., n,
V = the market value of the firm
S_{mv} = the market value of the equity
D_{mv} = the market value of the firm's borrowings
r = the overall cost of capital (required rate of return)
OR = the firm's operational receipts
OE = the firm's operational expenditure
I = the level of new investment
$\bar{x}$ = the firm's constant net operational cash flows $(OR - OE - I)$
ρ_k = the overall market capitalization rate depending upon the firm's risk class (k)
R_t = the firm's net operational cash flow in each future time-period $(OR - OE - I$, or $\bar{x}$ if a constant).

The above equations demonstrate the equivalence of modern approaches to the value of the firm, which is the sum of the market value of the company's ordinary shares plus the market value of the firm's borrowings, or the discounted future operational receipts less operational expenditures and new investment, or the capitalized future (constant) net operational cash flows, or the discounted net operational cash flows receivable in all future periods. The present value formula has been generally accepted for many years as a rational approach to company or project valuation. The formula does not make any reference to the financing of projects or the description of the net operational cash flows as dividends, retained earnings, or transfers to reserve, depreciation or deferred taxation.

Many traditional text books teach the present value approach to firm and project valuation in one chapter and then go on in later chapters to discuss the effects on firm valuation of leverage and dividend policies. The modern approach is consistent in that it teaches that the value of the firm is based on discounted net operational cash flows and that the value of the firm is not determined by leverage and dividend policies, at least in world with no taxation or transaction costs.

In an efficient market, two companies with identical investment schedules promising the same cash flows at the same level of risk must have exactly the same market value – regardless of the method of financing (ignoring the tax-deductibility of the interest on debt). Consider two companies with anticipated cash flows of £6,000 per annum in an industry risk class where anticipated cash flows are capitalized at 20 per cent (that is, multiplied by 5):

$$V = \frac{\bar{x}}{\rho_k} = \frac{£6,000}{0.2}, \text{ that is } \frac{\text{net operational cash flows}}{\text{capitalization rate}}$$

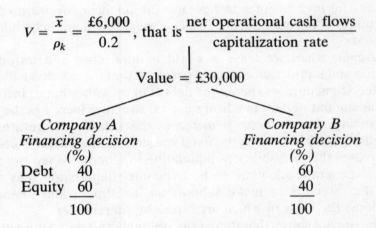

Value = £30,000

Company A Financing decision (%)		Company B Financing decision (%)
Debt	40	60
Equity	60	40
	100	100

The market value of the investment schedules must be identical at £30,000. Company A is financed by 40 per cent debt and 60 per cent equity, while Company B is financed by 60 per cent debt and 40 per cent equity. The financing decision, in the modern theory of finance, must be distinguished from the investment decision. Investment schedules are valued on the basis of operational cash flows and operational risk. Financing decisions in a world without taxation, transaction and bankruptcy costs do not influence the value of the investment schedule.

The traditional view has been that a company with a small amount of borrowing, say up to 30 per cent of total financing, has a lower average cost of capital than an unlevered company, because the required rate of return on debt is lower than the required rate of return on equity. For a given set of anticipated cash flows, the lower the average cost of capital, the higher is the market value. However, modern financial theory shows that if a levered company has a higher market value than an unlevered company with the same investment schedule, then a process akin to arbitrage takes place, whereby investors can switch from the levered company to the unlevered company and obtain the same level of cash flows for a lower investment or a higher level of cash flows for the same investment. Arbitrage prevents the same commodity, in this case operational cash flows, from selling in the same market at different prices. The traditional view that some optimal level of leverage (gearing) exists which minimizes the average rate of return and therefore maximizes the market value of the firm is based on confusion between operating decisions relating to the generation of a successful investment schedule and the financing decision which determines the method by which an investment schedule is financed.

Again, when we leave a world of innocence and introduce taxation and liquidation costs, we conclude that the tax-deductibility of interest encourages the use of debt. On the other hand, increasing the amount of debt in a firm's capital structure increases the risk to ordinary shareholders. It increases the volatility of returns to shareholders by increasing the fixed amounts of interest payable and it increases the probability of liquidation in a period when the firm fails to generate adequate cash. Impending liquidation may well lead the directors to make suboptimal investment and financing decisions, the costs of which are borne by shareholders.

Figure 5.4 shows that there is an optimal capital structure at the point where the market value of the firm is maximized. As interest is tax-deductible, after-tax cash flows are increased with borrowing, and therefore the market value of the firm with debt is greater than the all-equity value of the firm. This might appear to suggest that firms should finance themselves with 99 per cent debt. However, corporate managers do not do this because increasing the amount of debt also increases the financial risk, possibly to the point where liquidation may occur if the firm fails to generate adequate cash to make periodic interest payments. It should be stressed that the reason for the financial distress of the firm lies in unsuccessful investment policies, not financing policy. It is the failure of the

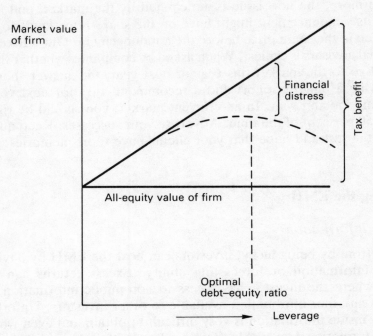

Figure 5.4   Leverage with corporation tax and liquidation costs

firm's investment schedule to generate adequate cash flows which results in corporate financial distress. The increasing probability of liquidation can result in costs, delays and the making of suboptimal investment decisions. There is therefore some optimal debt–equity ratio resulting from the trade-off between the tax benefit of increasing debt and the increasing probability of incurring the costs of financial distress. Efficient capital markets ignore neither financial risk nor economic risk. The portfolio manager should not expect that mechanical systems of investing in high-geared or low-geared companies will yield excess returns.

The timing of new issues

Companies often consult market specialists before deciding the date of a new issue or introduction of a new share to quotation. To the extent that an estimate of the future share price is relevant to the recommended issue date, the value of such advice must be questioned. The EMH suggests that it is extremely difficult to forecast the market price of a company's shares several months hence.

Furthermore, the new issue is anticipated by the market, and any effect its announcement might have on the share price tends to be reflected in the share price before the announcement. Our advice to financial advisers is cynical. When asked by companies whether they should go to the market this year or next year, the answer should always be a lengthy report and a recommendation for next year. Take the fee and wait. In an efficient market, you should be right about 50 per cent of the time. Advertise your successes. Keep quiet about the rest and hope that your clients have short memories.

Beating the EMH

Inside information

Apart from by being lucky, investors can beat the EMH by having inside information or forecasting ability. Excess returns can be made where the investor has access to non-public information as well as all other information available to other investors. Unfortunately, inside information is very difficult to obtain and even when such information is available there are legal pitfalls should the user of the information be discovered. Furthermore, the receiver of inside information must forecast correctly the effect of such information on share prices when the information becomes public. Monopolistic access to information apparently extends as far as specialists and corporate insiders. The performance of unit trusts suggests that their managers do not have access on a consistent basis to inside information.

Forecasting ability

If you feel that you can forecast general movements in the market, then you should hold a highly levered market portfolio or some other high-beta portfolio when you expect the market to move upwards. In an anticipated bear market, a low-beta portfolio should be held, or the investor could go completely liquid. Those investors who feel that they have forecasting expertise in some particular sector of the market should search out those companies with high levels of specific risk. Excess returns will be made if the investor can consistently identify those companies yielding returns greater than those predicted by the capital asset pricing model.

Other market inefficiencies

Inside information and forecasting ability may not be the only vehicles for achieving excess returns. In theory, financial markets will be efficient if a number of conditions including perfect information and absence of transaction costs are met. This suggests that where these conditions are not met, profitable opportunities may exist. Investors and their advisers should be aware of any market imperfections. For example, in countries with high marginal rates of tax, low-tax-rate investors may be wise to seek out high-yield shares which do not appeal to high-income investors. The annual capital gains tax exemption should not be overlooked. Investors should be aware that executors and trustees are not allowed to invest in companies which have recently passed a dividend. Such policies may lead to a market inefficiency. In the next chapter, we consider further research which suggests that the ideas of market efficiency which seemed so unassailable to academics in the late 1960s and early 1970s are by no means universally accepted in the 1990s.

Further reading

Brealey, R., and S. Myers: *Principles of Corporate Finance*, New York, McGraw-Hill, 1991, chapter 13.

6
The efficient market hypothesis revisited: some recent developments

Introduction

Chapter 4 described the development of the efficient market hypothesis in the 1960s, which gave rise to many studies that seemed almost unanimously to support the hypothesis. In 1978, Michael Jensen remarked at a seminar called to discuss market efficiency, 'I believe that there is no proposition in economics which has more solid evidence supporting it than the efficient market hypothesis' (Jensen, 1978, p. 95). In this chapter we shall review further research from the late 1970s to the present time. The more recent evidence suggests that the market is not as efficient as most academics once believed. The evidence falls into two parts. First, there are a number of apparent anomalies, and secondly, there is evidence which appears directly to refute the hypothesis.

The main anomalies which have been recorded in the literature include:

1 a size effect – that is, small companies have provided much higher returns than large companies;
2 a price–earnings (PE) ratio effect – companies with low PE ratios have given higher returns than those with high PE ratios;
3 a price to book value effect, whereby companies with a low price to book value ratio have shown excess returns;

4 a range of seasonal and calendar effects of which the most important is what has become known as the January effect; and finally,
5 a number of other anomalies which do not fall neatly into any of the above categories.

Many of these anomalies are closely related, and it is therefore often difficult to distinguish the effect of one anomaly from that of another.

A major difficulty in testing the efficient market hypothesis is that most tests are joint tests of market efficiency and of the capital asset pricing model (CAPM). So a test which rejects market efficiency may imply that the market is inefficient, or that the CAPM is flawed, or both. The reader will recall from chapter 3 that the CAPM predicts that a security's return depends on only two factors. First, there is the excess return on the market (the market return less the risk-free rate) and secondly, the security's systematic risk as measured by its β.

Anomalies

Size effect: Banz (1981)

Banz showed that firms which were small as measured by market capitalization had provided investors with much larger returns than large firms. Banz's sample included all common stocks which had been traded on the New York Stock Exchange (NYSE) for at least five years between 1926 and 1975. He calculated that the average excess returns from holding very small firms long and very large firms short over the period 1936–75 was 19.8 per cent on an annualized basis, a rate well above the average return on the market. This strategy, which suggests large profits, does, however, leave the investor with a poorly diversified portfolio. Banz found that the size effect was most pronounced for the smallest firms in his sample and also that it was not uniform throughout the period. He offered no conclusions as to why small firms should have given much larger returns than large firms, but suggested that his results might be due to a mis-specification of the CAPM rather than to market inefficiency.

A number of other researchers have confirmed the size effect in US markets. These include Reinganum (1981, 1982) and Blume and Stambaugh (1983).

Explanations of the size effect

Researchers have suggested the following explanations for the size effect:

1 Market liquidity. The really large gains from the size effect only seem to apply to the shares of the smallest companies. However, it would be difficult for medium or large institutions to buy or sell small companies' shares on a worthwhile scale without shifting the market price adversely against them.
2 Information. Small firms probably do not present information as frequently or of as high quality as large firms. Therefore their shares may be more risky than those of large firms. The costs of monitoring the performance of a large portfolio of small firms will be greater than those of monitoring a smaller portfolio of large firms.
3 Mis-estimates of beta. The sample of small firms' shares may include a disproportionately large number of firms which have recently fallen on hard times. The gearing of these firms may have risen as a result of their difficulties, and estimates of their betas, which are usually measured over a five-year period, may be understated. Furthermore, the shares of the smallest companies may be traded relatively infrequently, so their quoted closing prices may not reflect the price at which an actual trade would have taken place. This results in their share price movements appearing insensitive to market movements and again to unrealistically low estimates of their betas. If actual betas are higher than estimated betas, excess returns will have been overstated by the CAPM.
4 Transaction costs. Transaction costs of buying and selling the shares of small firms are higher than those of buying and selling the shares of large firms. This will reduce the apparent excess returns of small firms.

The size effect does not seem to be confined to US stock markets. Similar effects have been found in Australian markets by Brown, Kleidon and Marsh (1983), in Canadian markets by Berges, McConnell and Schlarbaum (1984), and in Japanese markets by Nakamura and Terada (1984). In a more recent study, covering the period from April 1961 to March 1985, Levis (1989) found a size effect on the London Stock Exchange (LSE). However, his observed size premium of 5.1 per cent per annum was considerably lower than that recorded for other markets. Whether this was due to the time-periods being dissimilar between the studies, to difficulties in measuring risk for small companies' shares on the LSE, or to sample selection problems, is not clear. Levis reported also that the size effect was related closely to a dividend yield effect and a PE effect.

The explanations for the size effect given above undoubtedly account for a part of the anomaly. It may represent an inefficiency in capital markets or, alternatively, the CAPM may be mis-specified. The size effect may not appear in the future, since a number of unit trusts have been formed to invest in the shares of small companies.

Reinganum (1981) has argued that the size effect seems closely related to another anomaly in capital markets, the PE effect.

Price–earnings ratios: Basu (1977)

There has for some time been a market folklore that the shares of companies with low price–earnings (PE) ratios may be undervalued. Basu carried out the first academic study which allowed for risk and avoided any survivorship bias. From his sample of over 1,400 firms which traded on the NYSE between September 1956 and August 1971, he found that companies with low PEs tended to produce higher returns than predicted.

Similar results, but using more recent data from both NYSE and American Stock Exchange (AMEX) firms, appear in Reinganum (1981). He presented evidence which suggests that the PE effect is a proxy for the size effect – in other words, the companies with high PE ratios tend to be small companies – whereas Basu (1977) had presented evidence that suggested that the size effect was an imperfect proxy for the PE effect. Clearly the two effects are closely related, and it is difficult to separate the impact of one from that of the other.

Price to book value: Rosenberg, Reid and Lanstein (1985)

Rosenberg, Reid and Lanstein (1985) examined a sample of 1,400 companies over the period 1980–4 and found that excess returns could be earned by investing in companies which had a low share price to book value ratio. (Book value is the shareholders' funds in the company's balance sheet, divided by the number of issued shares.) In many ways this conclusion is not surprising, given the results described above. All three groups of anomalies, the small firm effect, the PE effect and the book value effect, are linked by a common factor, the low market capitalizations of the companies in the samples.

Seasonal and calendar effects: The January effect and Rozeff and Kinney (1976)

Before academic studies had been carried out, a number of market professionals had noticed that stock market prices seemed to fall towards the end of the year and rise in January. The existence of such a regular movement would of course provide market participants with opportunities for profitable dealing. When informed of this, academics were at first sceptical. Initial statistical tests using return serial correlations confirmed their scepticism, as they failed to reveal any serial dependence in stock prices. It was only when researchers used more appropriate statistical tools that the anomaly became apparent.

Rozeff and Kinney conducted the first rigorous study which confirmed the existence of the January effect. They used analysis of variance techniques to examine the monthly returns on all stocks on the New York Stock Exchange from 1904 to 1974 and established that the average return in January amounted to 3.5 per cent. If these returns were repeated throughout the year and compounded, the annual return would be above 50 per cent. However, their research showed that average monthly returns for the remaining 11 months in the year were less than 1 per cent. When they divided their results into three sub-periods of 1904–28, 1929–40 and 1941–74, they found that the January effect appeared in each period. At the time, the Rozeff and Kinney research attracted relatively modest interest. However, it was the discovery of the small firm effect by Banz and the PE effect by Basu which provided motivation for further investigation into anomalies. Keim (1983), in studying the small firm effect, identified that of the extra return earned by the smallest firms, one-quarter was earned during the first five trading days of the year. It is also interesting to note that nearly 50 per cent of the size effect occurs in January so there is a clear relation between the size effect and the January effect.

Numerous other studies have documented the January effect. Examples are Roll (1983), Tinic and West (1984), DeBondt and Thaler (1985), Corhay, Hawawini and Michel (1988), Guletkin and Guletkin (1987) and Lakonishok and Smidt (1988).

Attempts to explain the January effect

Attempts to explain the January effect have largely concentrated on the tax loss hypothesis. Brown, Keim, Kleidon and Marsh (1983) argued that investors sell shares which have recently seen large falls, so that they may establish a tax loss. Small firms are likely to be candidates for tax loss selling, since the variance of their stock price movements is typically larger than that for large firms. An examination of the January effect in international markets provides useful insights into the tax loss selling hypothesis, as some countries have tax years which do not end on 31 December, while other countries do not tax capital gains. Is there a January effect in these markets? If there is, it suggests that factors other than tax loss selling must be at work.

Guletkin and Guletkin (1983) carried out just such an examination. They applied the Rozeff and Kinney methodology to the stock markets in 15 different countries, including the UK, which has a tax year end on 5 April, and Japan, which does not tax capital gains. In all the markets they studied, they found that returns were higher in January than in the rest of the year, and for most of the markets studied the January effect was larger than in the United States. The January effect seems to be present in most stock markets in the world, including those which do not tax capital gains. The tax loss selling hypothesis does not, therefore, appear to be a satisfactory explanation.

A number of authors have argued not only that the January effect may be an anomaly but also that it conflicts with the CAPM. Why should investors receive most of their returns in January and not be rewarded for the risk that they bear through the rest of the year? The January effect therefore remains an unexplained puzzle.

Other calendar anomalies

Many other calendar anomalies have been documented in recent years. These include regularities related to the time of the day, Harris (1986), the day of the week, Ball and Bowers (1988), Cross (1973), French (1980), Gibbons and Hess (1981), Jaffe and Westerfield (1985), Keim and Stambaugh (1984) and Lakonishok and Levi (1982), and the time of the month, Ariel (1987). In a major study using 90 years of daily data, Lakonishok and Smidt (1988) have confirmed the existence of pricing anomalies around the turn of the week, turn of the month and turn of the year, and around holidays.

Many of the calendar anomalies, other than the January effect, are very small. None of them can be expected to occur regularly, and the size of transaction costs prohibits most investors from profiting from these regularities. However, they still remain a puzzle, since a careful retiming of purchases or sales could be used by institutions and market professionals to profit from these anomalies.

Other anomalies: DeBondt and Thaler (1985); French and Roll (1986); and investment trusts

There is a large and growing body of literature which records a number of other anomalies to the EMH. The following is a brief summary of the most interesting findings.

There is also evidence in the cognitive psychology literature, which is discussed later in this chapter, which suggests that individuals, far from being rational, tend to overreact to recent events and news.

DeBondt and Thaler have argued that shares which have performed poorly in recent years are underpriced, since they are out of favour with investors, while those which have performed well are overpriced due to a contrasting over-enthusiasm. Using monthly data from the NYSE from January 1926 to December 1982, they formed portfolios of 'winners' and 'losers'. They found that loser portfolios outperformed the market on average by 19.6 per cent over a 36-month period while winner portfolios earned about 5 per cent less than the market over the same period. They also found that excess returns for losers occurred mainly in one month, January. Not all authorities agree with De Bondt and Thaler. For example, Zarowin (1989) argues that DeBondt and Thaler's conclusions have been overstated, since part of the effect may be attributable to losers being small companies which in any case may be expected to outperform the market.

In an efficient market, the market's volatility will depend on the quantity of economically significant news which is released. During 1968, the NYSE was closed on Wednesdays for a period to allow brokerages to catch up with paperwork. Provided the same amount of information was generated about fundamentals on Wednesday as on other days in the week, volatility ought to have been no different. French and Roll, however, found that volatility was in fact lower on the Wednesdays when the market was closed, which suggested that volatility was due to trading rather than to the release of information. The volatility of capital markets has received considerable attention in recent years and we shall return to this later.

The shares of investment trusts in both the UK and the US have traded at prices substantially different from the value of their net assets per share. This presents an apparent anomaly, since it is irrational for a bundle of stocks representing a given dividend stream to be traded at a different price from that of the same dividend stream flowing from individual stocks. The amount of the premium above, or the discount below, net asset value varies from trust to trust and over time. There have been examples of trusts whose shares have traded at over double their net asset value for short periods, while more commonly in the UK, investment trust shares have traded at prices some 20 per cent to 30 per cent below net asset value. This apparent anomaly represents an active research area, with recent contributions from Lee, Shleifer and Thaler (1991), Ammer (1990) and Levis and Thomas (1992).

Psychological issues

Economic theory has assumed that markets are dominated by participants who are rational and who have stable, well-defined preferences. Studies by psychologists have challenged this assumption and have shown under experimental conditions that decision-makers are frequently far from rational.

In the appendix to chapter 2 it was shown that the following behavioural assumptions must be satisfied in order to be certain that individuals are rational:

1 Comparability.
2 Transitivity.
3 Strong independence.
4 Measurability.
5 Ranking.

In addition, models of rational choice assume the principle of procedure invariance which requires that equivalent models of elicitation of responses yield the same preference order (Tversky, Slovic and Kahneman (1990), p. 204). Some examples which follow suggest that individuals reach decisions which breach the behavioural assumptions listed above.

Slovic and Lichenstein (1968)

In an early study, Slovic and Lichenstein found that both buying and selling prices of gambles were primarily determined by payoffs, whereas choices between gambles were primarily influenced by the probability of winning and losing. Thus, given the following choices:

	Payoff £
H bet: 28/36 chance to win £10	7.8
L bet: 3/36 chance to win £100	8.3

most subjects chose the H bet in preference to the L bet, preferring to accept a lower payoff, £7.8 for H compared with £8.3 for L, in return for a higher chance of winning. When the question was reformulated and the subjects asked to state their lowest selling price, the majority stated a higher price for the L bet than the H bet, reversing their preferred choice. This phenomenon is called preference reversal, and the example demonstrates a failure of either the transitivity or the independence axioms.

Later, Lichenstein and Slovic (1971, 1973) replicated these experiments with similar results. In one study, the subjects were experienced gamblers playing for real money on the floor of the Four Queens Casino in Las Vegas.

Grether and Plott (1979)

These findings created considerable controversy and motivated Grether and Plott to conduct a series of further experiments aimed at discrediting psychologists' work when applied to economics. By carefully designing their tests to allow for a number of objections raised to early research, for example that the researchers were psychologists (thereby creating suspicions and causing the subjects to behave in an unusual way), or that lack of incentives affected the response pattern, they hoped to show that preference reversal was irrelevant to modern economic theory. Their results, however, confirmed those of previous studies. Furthermore, the existence of preference reversal was somewhat more common among subjects responding to financial incentives. This result is inconsistent with the argument that agents would act differently when given the opportunity to make real gains or suffer real losses from their activities.

Grether and Plott argue:

Taken at face value the data are simply inconsistent with preference theory and have broad implications about research priorities within economics. The inconsistency is deeper than the mere lack of transitivity or even stochastic transitivity. It suggests that no optimization principles of any sort lie behind the simplest human choices and that uniformities in human choice behaviour may result from principles which are of a completely different sort from those generally accepted. (Grether and Plott (1979), p. 623)

McNeil, Pauker, Sox and Tversky (1982)

In a further study, by McNeil, Pauker, Sox and Tversky (1982), patients were given statistical information about the outcomes for two treatments of lung cancer. The statistics were presented to some patients in terms of mortality rates and to others in terms of survival rates. The respondents then indicated their preferred treatment. The information was presented as follows:

Problem 1 (Survival frame)
Surgery: Of 100 people having surgery, 90 live through the post-operative period, 68 are alive at the end of the first year and 34 are alive at the end of five years.

Radiation Therapy: Of 100 people having radiation therapy, all live through the treatment, 77 are alive at the end of one year and 22 are alive at the end of five years.

Problem 2 (Mortality frame)
Surgery: Of 100 people having surgery, 10 die during surgery or the post-operative period, 32 die by the end of the first year and 66 die by the end of five years.

Radiation Therapy: Of 100 people having radiation therapy, none die during treatment, 23 die by the end of one year and 78 die by the end of five years.

The reader will have noticed that the two problems are essentially the same. In the first case, the problem has been formulated by simply expressing the number of subjects who survive rather than die, and in the second by expressing the number who die rather than survive. However, this minor change in formulation produced a marked effect. The overall percentage of respondents who favoured radiation therapy rose from 18 per cent in the survival frame to 44 per cent in the mortality frame. Perhaps somewhat surprisingly, similar results were found when the experiment was repeated with experienced physicians and statistically sophisticated business students. This experiment demonstrates that the framing of the question has an important impact on the decisions which the subject makes, and provides an example of the failure of invariance.

Kahneman and Tversky (1973)

In a separate strand of research, Kahneman and Tversky investigated individuals' ability to make rational forecasts when faced with information of varying predictive potential. For example, if forecasters are asked to predict the actual scores of students in a test, say out of 30 marks, and are given information concerning the percentile into which each student falls, then the forecasts should be very accurate and should reflect the actual spread of marks. However, if some less reliable form of information is given to the forecasters, such as scores from tests of mental concentration or of sense of humour, then the rational approach is to base forecasts for each student on the mean score of the test. Thus the spread of the forecasts should not be wide. This is precisely what Tversky and Kahneman did. They asked subjects to predict the future grade point average (GPA) for each of ten students. The same three predictors were used, percentile scores for GPA, for a test of mental concentration and for a test of sense of humour. The results showed that forecasters made predictions from nearly useless information, data on sense of humour, that was almost as extreme in variation as that derived from a nearly perfect predictor. This pattern leads to systematic biases: forecasts that diverge the most from the mean will tend to be too extreme, implying that forecast errors are predictable and that forecasts could be improved.

We have therefore shown in a number of examples that under experimental conditions decision-makers frequently do not appear to make rational decisions. However, many financial economists have been reluctant to accept these findings. For example, Robert Merton has argued:

> Specifically the same sharp empirical findings of cognitive misperceptions have not (at least to my knowledge) been shown to apply to individual decision making *when an individual is permitted to interact with others (as a group) in analysing an important decision and when the group is repeatedly called upon to make similar types of important investment decisions. But this is of course exactly the environment in*

which professional investors make their stock market decisions. (Merton (1987), p. 96)

Alternatives to the efficient market model

Claims that the stock market is rational and that share prices represent the present values of expected future dividends seemed to differ widely from many investors' personal experiences. The high volatility of the market appears to bear little relation to underlying economic events. For example, as long ago as 1936 Keynes commented:

> Professional investment may be likened to those newspaper competitions in which the competitors have to pick out the six prettiest faces from a hundred photographs, the prize being awarded to the competitor whose choice most nearly corresponds to the average preferences of the competitors as a whole; so that each competitor has to pick, not those faces which he himself finds the prettiest, but those which he thinks likeliest to catch the fancy of other competitors, all of whom are looking at the problem from the same point of view. (Keynes (1936), p. 156)

More recently, the October 1987 crash, which did not seem to be associated with any major release of bad news, provides a further example which suggests that the market is far from rational. Readers may recall that after a period of 12 years of bull market, the UK stock exchange fell by one-third in three days. Similar falls occurred in most other world markets. How is it possible that in an efficient market which is supposed to reflect all published information such enormous changes can take place in market values without the apparent release of any significant news?

We must now examine alternative models of price formation which do not assume that the market is dominated by investors who at all times behave rationally.

Fashions and fads

If fashions and fads are present in a wide variety of human activities, why should they not be present in the stock market? Shiller (1984, 1988) gives examples of activities which seem to be influenced by fashions. He cites the current enthusiasm for jogging, which has only relatively recently become popular despite the fact that the benefits of regular exercise for health have been widely known for many years. Shiller argues that social movements may spread relatively rapidly or they may take years to permeate through society. He goes on to suggest that a fad or a fashion may spread in a similar way through the investment community. Good news about one stock may bring it to the attention of investors, causing a rise in its price. This may make some investors wealthy. Other investors may observe this and wish to participate in the game, causing a further increase in the price. Eventually, the price of a stock may cease to rise, other stocks becoming more fashionable, and the fad will come to an end.

Rational bubbles

A form of this argument suggests that a rational investor will purchase an asset at a price in excess of fundamental value if he believes that other speculators may purchase the asset at an even higher price. In this way, rational bubbles may exist. Of course, the normal expectation is that bubbles will eventually burst and the share price will fall rapidly towards fundamental value. Some commentators, however, have claimed that it is possible for a bubble never to burst if successive generations of investors enter the market hoping for further rises in the asset's price. Readers may believe they have seen signs of fads or even of rational bubbles in both stock and property markets.

Noise

Fisher Black (1986) has argued there are two types of traders at work in financial markets. First, there are information traders, who trade on information, and secondly, there are noise traders, who trade on noise. Noise is irrelevant or meaningless information occurring within desired information. If all agree on the consequences of new information, then prices may change without any trading. However, if there is little or no trading in individual shares, there can be no trading in unit trusts or derivatives. The whole structure of financial markets depends on relatively liquid markets in shares of individual firms. The prices of these shares depend on them being actively traded. Therefore the more noise trading there is, the more liquid markets will be. However, noise trading puts noise into market prices, causing them to depart from intrinsic values. Black argues that a degree of inefficiency is necessary for any market to be liquid. However, traders with information can never be sure whether they are trading on information or noise. The noise that noise traders put into stock prices will be cumulative, since a drunk tends to wander further and further from his starting point. The further a share price moves from its intrinsic value, the more the information traders will be tempted to enter the market. Thus the price of the share may revert towards its intrinsic value over time. However, since all prices are noisy, we can never be sure how far away any share's price is from its intrinsic value. While noise creates the opportunity to trade profitably, at the same time noise makes it difficult to trade profitably. Black argues that a market may be efficient even though a share's price differs from its fundamental value by a factor of as much as two. Noise will cause a share's price to appear like a random walk process with a non-zero mean. Even sophisticated traders may have difficulty in recognizing and exploiting substantial differences between price and intrinsic value.

We can therefore see that noise may cause share price movements to appear as if they are a random walk when they depart substantially from their intrinsic value. We have also seen that Shiller's 'fads' model may provide an alternative to the EMH. One of the marked features of the early efficient market literature was the absence of any alternative to the efficient market hypothesis. This effectively set a low benchmark for its acceptance. The question which then interested researchers was whether the early statistical tests which suggested that stock prices followed a random walk were powerful enough to discriminate between a genuine random walk and a slow mean reverting fads model of the type proposed by Shiller.

Power of the tests of the efficient market hypothesis

The reader will recall from chapter 4 that the early tests of the weak form of efficient market used return serial correlations to test whether a series was random. For example, Fama (1965) found that over periods of up to 30 days return serial correlations were almost zero. In other words, short-term movements in stock prices were approximately random.

Summers (1986) showed, by simulating a series of share prices which might be typical of a market which showed excess volatility or which overreacted to new information, that the early tests lacked the power to discriminate between his simulated series and a random series. Under his assumptions, which have not been seriously challenged in the literature, it would be necessary to have stock market data for just over 5,000 years to be able to make this discrimination.

Summers argued:

> This means that the evidence found in many studies that the hypothesis of efficiency cannot be rejected should not lead us to conclude that market prices represent rational valuations. . . . The standard theoretical argument is that unless securities are priced efficiently, there will be opportunities to earn excess returns. Speculators will take advantage of the opportunities by arbitraging away any efficiencies in the pricing of securities. The argument does not explain how speculators became aware of profit opportunities. The same problems of identification described here which confront financial economists also plague would-be speculators. (Summers (1986), p. 20)

We therefore see that the evidence described in chapter 4 which generally strongly supports the weak and semi-strong versions of the EMH is weaker than originally thought. However, while the evidence is weaker, it is still consistent with the EMH. Stock prices are approximately a random series and information is quickly incorporated into share prices.

So far, we have considered a number of studies which reveal apparent anomalies in stock prices. We have also considered an alternative hypothesis that fads may influence prices in the same way as they appear to influence many other aspects of life. Finally, we have considered the contribution of Summers, who showed that many of the early statistical tests were not sufficiently powerful to discriminate between the two hypotheses.

We must now turn to consider a parallel development in the study of stock market behaviour, that involving the alleged excess volatility of stock market prices.

Excess volatility

Many casual observers have commented on the apparent implausibility of the EMH, since stock prices seem to be very volatile. A reference has already been made to the Keynes beauty contest analogy and to the October 1987 crash. The question which faced researchers was how could the stock market be so volatile if it represented an optimal forecast of anticipated future dividends discounted at shareholders' required rates of return? The series of dividends appeared to be relatively smooth when compared with the apparently wild fluctuations in stock market prices. This led to a number of studies which tested whether share prices were more volatile than justified by dividends.

The intuition behind these tests is simple. Suppose in a game of chance we know that the mean score will be 60 and the standard deviation of possible outcomes is 10. Our best forecasts for repeated trials will of course be 60, and the standard deviation of successive forecasts will be zero. However, we also know that the standard deviation of actual outcomes will be above zero. Thus, given uncertainty in the stock market over the future levels of dividends, prices, in an efficient market, ought to be less volatile than the present value of actual dividends.

One of the features of an optimal forecast is that forecast errors should be uncorrelated. Suppose this year I attempt to forecast next year's share price, and I continue to do this each year in succession. If my forecasts are biased for any reason, I may underestimate prices for a number of years and then in later years I may overestimate prices. These forecast errors will show serial correlation, and my forecasting model should be capable of improvement. However, we know from previous chapters that today's stock prices are, in an efficient market, optimal forecasts of future stock prices.

Shiller 1981

Shiller (1981a) attempted to test this proposition rigorously. The efficient market model can be described as asserting that:

$$p_t = E_t(p_t^*) \tag{6.1}$$

where p_t is a stock price index and p_t^* is the present value of actual dividends. In other words, p_t is an optimal forecast of p_t^*. As discussed in the last paragraph of the previous section, the error term, $\mu_t = p_t - p_t^*$, must be uncorrelated with the forecast. If this is so, the covariance of p_t and μ_t must be zero. Therefore, $\mathrm{Var}(p^*) = \mathrm{Var}(\mu) + \mathrm{Var}(p)$. Since variances are positive, $\mathrm{Var}(p) \leqslant \mathrm{Var}(p^*)$, or $\sigma(p) \leqslant \sigma(p^*)$. This again demonstrates the principle that a forecast, which in this case is the actual stock price, should be less volatile than the item forecast, the discounted dividend stream.

Shiller compared the volatility of an actual series of dividends which he discounted at a constant interest rate, what he called the perfect foresight price, with the volatility of actual prices and found that a stock price index from 1871 to 1979 was over five times more volatile, in terms of standard deviation, than allowed by his variance bounds test. Le Roy and Porter (1981) carried out slightly different tests but again found excess volatility.

Shiller's (1981a) test of excess volatility was criticized by a number of authors, for example Flavin (1983), Kleidon (1986) and Marsh and Merton (1986), on grounds of alleged econometric shortcomings. However, his tests were replicated in a number of further, more sophisticated, studies which overcame these econometric objections. These tests still showed excess volatility, but at a lower level. Another criticism of Shiller's work was that discount rates may not stay constant but may change in line with economic conditions and perceived risks of stock market investment. Shiller (1988) and West (1988) have argued that the amount of change in the discount rate necessary to account for the excess volatility is implausibly large. Cochrane (1991), on the other hand, disagreed, and demonstrated with a simple model how small changes to the discount rate could make large changes to a share's price. Cochrane argues that since the risk premium, the excess of the required rate of return over the risk-free rate, is unknown, we can expect large fluctuations in share prices.

A further, and less technical, explanation of excess volatility is that the stock market may be concerned from time to time with the consequences of a dramatic event of low probability, for example a major collapse of the prosperity of Western economies. Shiller (1981b) argues that the probability of such a dramatic event would have to change dramatically from one period to another to account for the excess volatility of the market. There certainly is no evidence of such a disaster having occurred in Shiller's sample of over 100 years of US data.

Bulkey and Tonks (1989)

Relatively little work on excess volatility has been carried out in the UK. An exception is the study by Bulkey and Tonks (1989), who again found excess volatility. These authors developed a trading rule which capitalized on this to bring modest post-tax excess returns of 1.5 per cent annum.

The finding of alleged excess volatility led to the conclusion that returns on the stock market and on bonds might be forecastable. Any ability to forecast returns on the market might suggest that profitable trading rules exist which would represent market inefficiency. Alternatively, an ability to forecast returns might be consistent with a market in which the risk premium which investors expect to receive for holding equities changes in a rational manner with business conditions. In other words, while investors may be able to predict increased returns, these increased returns represent compensation for the additional risk of equity investment.

Mean reversion

The finding of excess volatility seemed to imply that if share prices were too high or too low in relation to their intrinsic value, they would, in time, revert to a mean along the trend of their price series. Such mean reversion implies negative serial correlation in the time series of stock returns over a long period, say over two years, and in a world of constant discount rates, is consistent with a fads model such as those of Shiller and Summers.

Poterba and Summers (1988)

Poterba and Summers decided to use a recently developed technique known as variance ratios to test whether serial correlations of stock returns on the NYSE from 1926 to 1985 were in fact zero. They found some evidence of positive correlations of returns for periods of under one year but more substantial evidence of negative correlations for periods of over two years. This suggests that stock prices may revert to a mean over long periods.

The authors also examined mean reversion in stock price indices in 17 other countries. Canadian data were taken from the period since 1919, data for the UK from the period since 1939 and data for the 15 other countries from a shorter post-war period. Most countries displayed negative serial correlation for long-horizon returns, except for South Africa, Spain and Finland.

However, it will be recalled that any test of market efficiency is a joint test of efficiency and of the model specifying equilibrium required returns. Thus mean reversion may again be the result of time varying discount rates. To investigate the changes in discount rates necessary to explain their results, Poterba and Summers calculated, for a wide range of assumptions, the standard deviation in the required rates of return. They found that, under what they considered to be reasonable assumptions, the standard deviation of *ex ante* returns must be 5.8 per cent per annum, and they argue that it is difficult to think of risk factors which could account for such a large variation in discount rates.

Poterba and Summers conclude that their tests of a number of data sets strengthen the case against the random walk hypothesis. They argue that the presence of transitory price components suggests the desirability of investment strategies, such as those considered by De Bondt and Thaler (1985), involving the purchase of securities which have recently declined in value.

Fama and French (1988a)

The finding of transitory components in stock prices led to a more direct test of return serial correlation by Fama and French, who again showed that returns on the NYSE had a mean reverting component. However, a caveat is necessary at this stage. The authors found strong evidence of negative serial correlation in the first 15 years covered by their survey, from 1926 to 1940. The serial correlations for the period after 1941 were close to zero, suggesting that the negative correlations occurred only in the early period, which encompassed the stock market crash of 1929.

The empirical evidence of excess volatility and mean reversion both seemed to support Shiller's fads model. However, shortly after the publication of the research by Poterba and Summers (1988) and Fama and French (1988a), Cecchetti, Lam and Mark (1990) challenged the findings of mean reversion, arguing that much of the serial correlation in historical stock returns could be attributed to small-sample bias.

Return forecasting regressions

The evidence of mean reversion and excess volatility suggested that returns on the stock market could be forecast. However, while the ability to predict future returns might be interpreted as evidence of market inefficiency since it could lead to profitable trading rules, it could also be attributed to predictable changes in the interest rate at which investors discount cash flows.

Fama and French (1988b)

In a further test, Fama and French examined whether it was possible to forecast returns on the NYSE for horizons from one month to four years using dividend yield as the explanatory variable. They found considerable success in predicting returns for periods of two or four years ahead. They agreed that their results were consistent with common models of an inefficient market, for example those of Shiller (1984) and Summers (1986), in which stock prices take long temporary swings away from fundamental values. A high dividend yield may signal that future returns will be high because stock prices are temporarily irrationally low, and a low dividend yield may indicate that prices are irrationally high. However, Fama and French also pointed out that their results were equally consistent with a world in which investors are changing their discount rates in line with their shifting perceptions of risk. The question which now faced Fama and French was whether this mean reversion might be due to changes in business conditions and whether similar economic factors affected the returns on bonds as well as on stocks.

Fama and French (1989)

Fama and French, in the last of a series of studies, found that returns on stocks and low-grade bonds moved together and also that a number of economic variables such as dividend yields and the default spread, which is the difference between the return on high-grade and low-grade corporate bonds, forecast the returns on both stocks and bonds. The dividend yield and the default spread both predict high returns when business conditions are persistently weak and low returns when business conditions are strong.

The regressions showed very considerable success in forecasting returns on both stocks and low-grade bonds for periods from one year to four years ahead. This by itself might suggest market inefficiencies and potential for profitable trading rules. However, the authors argue that the evidence provided by their study suggests that the forecasting variables, which are related to business conditions, track a common variation in the returns on stocks and bonds. They also argue that it is comforting that the variation in dividend yield, which might otherwise be interpreted as the result of bubbles in stock prices, forecasts bond returns as well as stock returns.* They argue that their results are consistent with a world in which changing business conditions may affect the rate at which shareholders discount anticipated cash flows from stocks and bonds.

More recently, Kim, Nelson and Startz (1991) have shown that the statistical significance of the return forecasting regressions of Fama and French may be lower than estimated by the authors. We therefore see some weak evidence that returns on shares may be forecast, which suggests profitable trading rules. Whether profits gained from such trading rules represent genuine economic profits or whether they are merely a compensation for additional risk is a topic still generating considerable controversy in academic journals.

Alternatives to the capital asset pricing model

In the previous section we stressed that most tests of market efficiency are joint tests of market efficiency and the model specifying equilibrium returns, the CAPM. We must now consider briefly two other asset pricing models which appear in the literature. They are the arbitrage pricing model (APT) and the consumption capital asset pricing model (CCAPM).

Arbitrage pricing model

Following the Roll critique of the CAPM which was described in chapter 3, Stephen Ross (1976) developed Arbitrage Pricing Theory (APT). APT states that a stock's return depends on its sensitivity to

---

* However, a possible explanation might be that the variation in dividend yields is caused by the same overreaction by investors which causes bond yields to vary.

a number of macroeconomic factors. Thus the return can be stated as:

$$\text{Return} = a + \beta_1(\text{factor 1}) + \beta_2(\text{factor 2}) + \ldots + \beta_n(\text{factor n}).$$
$$(6.2)$$

While it is possible for the individual investor to eliminate unique risk by diversification, it is not possible for the investor to diversify away a share's exposure to a variety of macroeconomic factors. These factors appear in equation (6.2) above. The beta coefficients will vary from share to share depending on the share's exposure to each factor.

The advantage of APT compared with the CAPM is that the CAPM depends on the identification of the market portfolio while APT makes no such assumption. As was explained in chapter 3, it is not possible to identify the market portfolio precisely, since it should include the prices of all assets, not just those of securities quoted on stock markets. A major disadvantage of the APT is that the theory gives no insights into what the macroeconomic factors might be. There have been a number of attempts to test APT. One class of tests uses factor analysis. This attempts to identify first whether a number of common factors which determine stock returns are present in the data and secondly what weights to give to each of these factors. Roll and Ross (1980) carried out such a test and found that there are three or possibly four factors in stock returns which appear to be significantly priced. However, while the technique may identify common factors, the factors are in essence statistical artifacts and may not have any direct economic interpretation. This severely limits the usefulness of these tests. An alternative approach has been adopted by Chen, Roll and Ross (1986) to test whether a number of factors which are suggested by economic theory are priced. Their results showed that the following macroeconomic variables were important:

1 An index of industrial production.
2 Changes in default risk premium.
3 Changes in the yield curve.
4 Unanticipated inflation.

However, Poon and Taylor (1991) have criticized this study on econometric grounds, and their attempt to replicate it, using UK data, proved unsuccessful. While APT has a number of theoretical attractions, the inability to determine what factors should be included in the model severely limits its practical application.

Consumption capital asset pricing model (CCAPM)

Economists such as Breeden (1979) have argued that instead of maximizing wealth, individuals may try to maximize lifetime consumption. If this is the case, the most important risks are those which affect future consumption. They therefore propose a model in which return on an asset is linearly related to the growth rate of aggregate consumption. In such a model, a firm's beta is measured by the sensitivity of its returns to changes in aggregate consumption.

However appealing from a theoretic viewpoint this model may be, there are severe problems in measuring consumption changes over time. The volatility of consumption appears too low to explain past returns on shares, and empirical tests of the CCAPM have shown mixed results.

Summary

The remark made by Michael Jensen in 1978 quoted at the beginning of this chapter, that there is no proposition in economics which has more solid evidence supporting it than the efficient market hypothesis, in retrospect provides a high water mark to the notion that the market is rational.

Since 1978, a considerable body of evidence has been uncovered that casts doubts on the validity of the EMH. Perhaps it is not surprising that, given the power and simplicity of the EMH, it has been subject to many hundreds of tests, and that some of these have uncovered evidence which does not support the hypothesis. However, there are a number of reasons for not abandoning the EMH:

1 There are strong *a priori* reasons for believing stock markets to be efficient. There are a large number of participants competing for gains, transaction costs are generally small, and information on companies' profitability and financial health is widely available.
2 Despite Summers' criticisms of the power of many of the early tests, there is an enormous body of evidence from event studies which shows that stock prices respond rapidly to the release of new information.
3 Many of the calendar anomalies that were discussed earlier are small, and only market professionals are likely to be able to profit from them. It is possible that the availability of cheap and powerful computing will

make it easy in the future to detect such anomalies. However, such detection will lead to their immediate disappearance.

4 The evidence of excess volatility seemed at first to provide a powerful refutation of the EMH. However, econometric shortcomings in the early work, as well as revised tests, suggest that the evidence of excess volatility is less convincing than at first appeared. The same applies to studies of mean reversion and return forecasting regressions.

5 If we ignore the EMH, we must ask ourselves what alternative hypothesis explains stock prices, and how far the evidence supports this alternative. If fashions or fads affect stock prices, it would be useful to have a model which explained why fads occur, when they occur, how large they should be and how long they should last.

6 If non-rational models, such as those involving fads and fashions suggested by DeBondt and Thaler, Shiller and Summers, more effectively describe the market than the EMH, it still may be difficult and risky for traders to develop profitable trading rules.

In real life, financiers need a model to guide their decisions. The efficient market hypothesis may not be a perfect description of how stock prices are formed. The interesting issue is whether, in the light of the evidence which weakens support for the EMH, decision-makers should use an alternative hypothesis to the EMH and, if so, what this hypothesis should be. It is clear that the EMH has come of age. How far financiers will be able to rely on the implications of the efficient market will be a subject for continued debate in years to come.

Further reading

Dimson, E.: *Stock Market Anomalies*, Cambridge, Cambridge University Press, 1988.

Fama, E.: Efficient Capital Markets II. *Journal of Finance*, 46, December 1991, pp. 1575–1617.

LeRoy, S.: Efficient Capital Markets and Martingales. *Journal of Economic Literature*, 27, 1989, pp. 1583–1621.

Mills, T.: *Predicting the Unpredictable?* London, Institute of Economic Affairs, Occasional Paper 87, October 1992.

Shiller, R.: *Market Volatility*, Cambridge, Mass., and London, MIT Press, 1989.

7

Risk measurement services

Available risk measurement services

Organizations which provide risk measurement services (or beta services) on a regular basis exist in several countries. Although these organizations tend to use similar methods, they do differ in emphasis. Most use past price changes to form estimates, but some also incorporate historical data from companies' balance sheets and income statements. In addition, procedures differ. The various risk measurement services calculate β values using different lengths of time-period, different observation frequencies and different market indices. The estimated β values for a given security obtained by different organizations should therefore not be expected to be exactly the same.

The London Business School's *Risk Measurement Service*

In the UK, a major institution which provides risk measures is the London Business School (LBS), through its *Risk Measurement Service* (*RMS*) publication. Each quarter, the *RMS* publishes estimates of the variability of approximately 2,000 British shares. Each share's variability is also split into two parts – that which stems from general market movements (market risk), and that which is specific to a particular share (specific risk). These measures are based on an analysis of share price movements over the previous five years, using data collected at monthly intervals. Thus, in general, each estimate is based on 60 observations. In addition to risk measures, the *RMS* provides data on returns, and further financial information on companies is also tabulated.

In the following discussion of risk measurement, the *RMS* will be used for illustrative purposes. Much of the information is obtained from Dimson and Marsh (1979), (1982), and Marsh (1980).

Measuring the risk and return of individual shares

Estimation of market model

The LBS's *RMS* estimates risk using historical share price data only. The market model (3.1) developed in chapter 3 is

$$R_i = \alpha_i + \beta_i R_M + U_i$$

where R_i is the return of the ith security, R_M is the return of the market portfolio, α_i and β_i are parameters, and U_i is a random error term which is assumed to satisfy the usual properties required by the classical linear regression model. The monthly returns (dividend yield plus capital appreciation) are calculated for each share, and also the corresponding returns for the market index. The *Financial Times* all-share index, which accounts for approximately 90 per cent of the UK market by value, is used as an approximation for the market index. An ordinary least-squares regression of the return of the ith security on the market return yields estimates of the coefficients α and β for the ith security, which may be denoted by $\hat{\alpha}_i$ and $\hat{\beta}_i$, respectively.

The values estimated for α and β may differ substantially from the true values on account of statistical measurement difficulties. The extent of potential error can be measured, however, and a range derived within which the true parameter value is almost certain to lie. This is accomplished by using 'standard errors'. For example, the *RMS* publishes the standard error (SE) associated with each estimated β coefficient. It is approximately 95 per cent certain that the true β value will lie between the limits

$$\hat{\beta} \pm 2SE(\hat{\beta}).$$

This range centres on the value estimated for β, and the lower the SE, the more confidence we have in our $\hat{\beta}$ value. A low SE implies a narrow range within which the true β is likely to lie.

The goodness of fit of the regression line estimated from equation (3.1) may be measured by the coefficient of determination (adjusted for degrees of freedom), denoted by $\bar{R}^2$. The latter shows the proportion of the variance of the return of the ith security which is explained by the estimated characteristic line. The closer the $\bar{R}^2$ value is to unity, the higher is the explanatory power of the model, and the greater the extent to which total security risk is determined by market risk.

Tabulated risk measures

The *variability* of a share is measured by the standard deviation of the returns of the share, and indicates the total risk attaching to the share. The variabilities of UK shares lie within the range 20 per cent per annum to 110 per cent per annum, with an average value of 31 per cent (see Dimson and Marsh (1982)). Variabilities may be interpreted as direct measures of downside risk. The annual return of the share will fall short of its expected value by at least its variability in approximately one year out of six.

The variance of the returns of share i, $V(R_i)$, may be split into systematic and unsystematic parts. Equation (3.3) shows that

$$V(R_i) = \beta_i^2 V(R_M) + V(U_i)$$

where $V(R_M)$ is the variance of the market return, and $V(U_i)$ is the variance of the error term. The expression $\beta_i^2 V(R_M)$ denotes the systematic risk component, and $V(U_i)$ the unsystematic risk component, of total variance. If the standard deviation of return is taken to measure risk, then the market risk of security i is given by $\beta_i \sigma_M$, where σ_M is the standard deviation of the market return. Now, as discussed in chapter 3, the σ_M term is common to all securities, so the market risk of security i can be thought of in relative terms – that is, merely in terms of β_i. Hence, beta represents the market risk component of total risk. Equation (3.1) shows that beta measures the sensitivity of the return of the share to general market movements. For example, if $\beta = 1.5$, then the return of the share tends to change by 1.5 per cent when the market return changes by 1 per cent.

The second component of variability is *specific risk*, and from equation (3.3) this is calculated as the standard deviation of the error term. Specific risk represents that part of the risk of the share which is unrelated to market fluctuations. Even if the market return were constant, the annual return of the share would fall short of its expected value by at least its specific risk in approximately one year out of six. For individual shares, specific risk is the more important component of total risk, typically accounting for approximately two-thirds of the share's variability. Most of the specific risk of shares is eliminated in a diversified portfolio, however, so in this situation beta becomes by far the more important component.

In addition to the three risk measures – variability, beta and specific risk – the *RMS* tabulates the *standard error* and $\bar{R}^2$. The standard error refers to $SE(\hat{\beta})$, and may be used to construct confidence intervals for beta, as already discussed. $\bar{R}^2$ measures the extent to which market risk accounts for total security risk, and has also been discussed earlier.

Tabulated return measures

The *annual actual return* measures the percentage capital appreciation plus dividend yield over the previous year. Gross dividends are assumed to be reinvested in the share at the end of the month in which they are paid.

The *quarterly/annual abnormal return* measures the performance of the share over the previous quarter/year, relative to the market as a whole, and corresponds to the concept of 'risk-adjusted excess return' discussed in chapter 3. The abnormal return is equal to the difference between the actual return of a share and the return which could have been obtained over the same period from an investment in a diversified portfolio with the same beta. Rewriting equation (3.28) in terms of an individual security i gives

$$\bar{\alpha}_i^* = \bar{R}_i - \bar{R}_s \tag{7.1}$$

where $\bar{\alpha}_i^*$ is the abnormal return, $\bar{R}_i$ is the realized rate of return of security i, and $\bar{R}_s$ is the realized rate of return of the performance standard. Hence, if equation (3.31) is rewritten in terms of a single security, the following is obtained:

$$\bar{\alpha}_i^* = \alpha_i - \bar{R}_F(1 - \beta_i) \tag{7.2}$$

where α_i and β_i are estimated from the market model (3.1), and $\bar{R}_F$ is the realized rate of return of the risk-free asset. If a positive abnormal return is estimated for a security over a given time-period, then it has outperformed the market during that period, whereas a negative abnormal return implies that the security has underperformed.

Regression bias

A share's β value may be estimated from equation (3.1) using regression analysis. In the absence of any further information, this is the best estimate of the true β value. However, additional information is available, since the average β value is 1.0 by definition. Furthermore, it has been shown that betas are approximately normally distributed with a standard deviation of 0.3 (see Cunningham (1973)). Hence, about 95 per cent of shares have betas which lie between 0.4 and 1.6 (that is, within the range $\hat{\beta} + 2SE(\hat{\beta})$). This additional information may be used to adjust the β values yielded by regression. Using Bayesian statistics, the original β estimate may be adjusted on the basis of prior knowledge about the cross-sectional distribution of the betas and the standard error of the estimate. The net result of the adjustment is to move all β estimates towards the mean value of 1.0. Similarly, other risk measures should be Bayesian-adjusted. All the *RMS* measures are modified in this manner to remove regression bias (for a description of the methods used, see, for example, Vasicek (1973)).

Example

The risk and return measures may be illustrated by examining figures from the *RMS*. Table 7.1 shows the values for the shares of three companies as published in the July 1982 *RMS*. Examination of the figures for Hill (P.) Inv. Tr. plc shows that the total risk attaching to its shares, as indicated by variability, is 24 per cent. Hence, in approximately one year out of six the annual return of a share in this company will fall short of its expected value by at least 24 per cent. The beta value of 1.08 denotes the market risk component of total risk, and indicates that a 1 per cent change in the market return is associated with a 1.08 per cent change in the return of a share in Hill (P.) Inv. Tr. plc. Thus the return of the share tends to change almost in line with changes in the market return. The specific risk figure of 11 per cent shows that even if the market return did not fluctuate, in approximately one year out of six the annual return of the share would fall short of its expected value by at least 11 per cent. For this company the specific risk is less than one-half of total risk, which is a relatively low figure, suggesting that the company is itself well diversified. From the standard error figure, it can be seen that it is approximately 95 per cent certain that

Table 7.1   Risk and return measures for selected companies

Company name	Stock exchange industry classification	Variability (%)	Beta	Specific risk (%)	Standard error	R^2 (%)	Annual actual return (%)	Quarterly abnormal return (%)	Annual abnormal return (%)
Hill (P.) Inv. Tr. plc	Investment trust	24	1.08	11	0.07	77	9	2	2
Holt (Joseph) Ltd	Brewery	28	0.28	27	0.19	7	80	51	70
Ibstock Johnsen	Bricks and roofing tiles	36	1.39	23	0.13	59	−7	−9	−11

Source: Dimson and Marsh (1982).

the true β value will lie within the range 0.94 to 1.22. As the range is fairly narrow, we have considerable confidence in our estimated value for β. The $\bar{R}^2$ value indicates that 77 per cent of the variance of the return of the security is explained by the estimated characteristic line. This is a relatively high value, showing that the explanatory power of the model is good. The actual return of a share in Hill (P.) Inv. Tr. plc was 9 per cent over the previous year. The abnormal return figures show that over both the previous quarter and the previous year the company's shares outperformed the market by 2 per cent; that is, the actual return of a share was 2 per cent higher than the return of the performance standard.

Investment trusts tend to be well-diversified companies as they generally have wide holdings of securities. Usually, specific risk is therefore low and the $\bar{R}^2$ value high. Furthermore, most well-diversified companies have beta values close to unity. In addition, the absolute values of the abnormal returns are likely to be low for companies with low specific risks. The figures for the risk and return measures for Hill (P.) Inv. Tr. plc which appear in table 7.1 therefore support expectations. Similarly, the returns associated with shares in breweries are not expected to vary greatly with general stock market movements, and the data tabulated for Holt (Joseph) Ltd show this to be the case. The low value obtained for beta, 0.28, shows that the return of a share in this company is very unresponsive to changes in the market return. Most of the variability of the share (28 per cent) is made up of specific risk (27 per cent), which results in the high standard error and low $\bar{R}^2$ values recorded. Not surprisingly, the absolute values of the abnormal return figures are high. Finally, the return of a share in Ibstock Johnsen, a company in the bricks and roofing tiles industry, is expected to respond in a highly volatile manner to general stock market movements. This is supported by an estimated beta value of 1.39, with a 95 per cent confidence interval for β of 1.13 to 1.65. It is therefore almost certain that the true β value exceeds unity.

Measuring the risk and return of portfolios

Portfolio risk and return may be estimated either directly or indirectly. The former method involves using historical returns data for the actual portfolio to estimate the portfolio's characteristic line. The risk and return measures for the portfolio may then be calculated in exactly the same manner as the corresponding measures for an individual share.

It is much more common to estimate portfolio risk and return from information on the constituent shares of the portfolio. Equation (3.11) indicates that the β factor of a portfolio is equal to a weighted average of those of the individual securities:

$$\beta_p = \sum_{i=1}^{n} X_i \beta_i$$

where β_p is the beta of the portfolio, β_i is the beta of security i, X_i is the proportion of the market value of the portfolio invested in security i, and n, is the number of securities in the portfolio. Thus, using the beta values for individual shares published in the *RMS*, it is possible to calculate the portfolio beta factor.

The measurement of the specific risk of a portfolio is somewhat more complicated. However, if the portfolio is fairly well diversified, so that it is reasonable to assume that the only link among the constituent shares is through their tendency to move with the market, then the specific risk of a portfolio may be calculated approximately from the specific risk figures for the individual shares. Equation (2.10) states that

$$V(R) = \sum_{i=1}^{n} X_i^2 \sigma_i^2 + 2 \sum_{i=1}^{n-1} \sum_{j=i+1}^{n} X_i X_j \rho_{ij} \sigma_i \sigma_j$$

where $V(R)$ is the variance of return of the portfolio, σ_i^2 is the variance of return of security i, X_i is the proportion of security i in the portfolio, ρ_{ij} is the correlation coefficient between the returns of securities i and j, and n is the number of securities in the portfolio. Hence, the specific risk of a portfolio is given by

$$(\sigma_p^u)^2 = \sum_{i=1}^{n} X_i^2 (\sigma_i^u)^2 \qquad (7.3)$$

where σ_p^u is portfolio unsystematic risk and σ_i^u is the unsystematic risk of security i. As the returns of the shares in the portfolio are uncorrelated (apart from their tendency to move with the market), the correlation coefficients in equation (2.10) all reduce to zero in equation (7.3). Clearly, if the portfolio exhibits any industry concentration, say, equation (7.3) will tend to underestimate portfolio specific risk. Equation (7.3) permits the calculation of portfolio specific risk from the specific risk figures for individual securities published in the *RMS*.

Portfolio variability may be calculated from a knowledge of the market risk and specific risk of the portfolio. Rewriting equation (3.3) in terms of a portfolio of securities gives

$$V(R_p) = \beta_p^2 V(R_M) + V(U_p) \tag{7.4}$$

where $V(R_p)$ is the variance of return of the portfolio, $\sqrt{[\beta_p^2 V(R_M)]}$ is the market risk of the portfolio, and $\sqrt{[V(U_p)]}$ is the specific risk of the portfolio. Equation (7.4) may thus be restated as

$$\text{(Portfolio variability)}^2 = \text{(Portfolio market risk)}^2$$
$$+ \text{(Portfolio specific risk)}^2. \tag{7.5}$$

The variability of a portfolio may therefore be calculated once the beta value and specific risk of the portfolio are known. The only additional information required is the variability of the market index, $\sigma_M = \sqrt{[V(R_M)]}$.

Example

The following example shows how the risk and return measures for individual securities given in the *RMS* may be used to calculate the corresponding measures for portfolios. It is supposed that a portfolio comprises holdings in the three companies listed in table 7.1 in the proportions given in table 7.2.

The three risk measures, variability, beta and specific risk, are calculated as follows. The beta of the portfolio, β_p, is obtained by substituting into equation (3.11):

$$\beta_p = \sum_{i=1}^{n} X_i \beta_i$$
$$= (0.5)(1.08) + (0.4)(0.28) + (0.1)(1.39)$$
$$= 0.79.$$

Table 7.2 Portfolio composition (example)

Company name	Fraction of portfolio
Hill (P.) Inv. Tr. plc	0.5
Holt (Joseph) Ltd	0.4
Ibstock Johnsen	0.1

Thus the market risk of the portfolio is 0.79 times the risk of the *Financial Times* all-share index. Now the values for the risk measures tabulated in the *RMS* imply that the variability of the index is 20 per cent, and so the market risk of the portfolio is $(0.79)(20) = 16$ per cent. The specific risk of the portfolio, σ_p^u, is given by substituting into equation (7.3):

$$(\sigma_p^u)^2 = \sum_{i=1}^{n} X_i^2(\sigma_i^u)^2$$

$$= (0.5)^2(11)^2 + (0.4)^2(27)^2 + (0.1)^2(23)^2$$

$$= 152.$$

Therefore

$$\sigma_p^u = 12 \text{ per cent.}$$

Finally, the variability of the portfolio, $S(R_p)$, may be calculated by substituting the appropriate values into equation (7.5):

$$[S(R_p)]^2 = (\text{Portfolio market risk})^2$$
$$+ (\text{Portfolio specific risk})^2$$
$$= 250 + 152$$
$$= 402.$$

Therefore

$$S(R_p) = 20 \text{ per cent.}$$

$\overline{R}^2$, which shows the proportion of the variance of the return of the portfolio that is accounted for by its market risk component, is given by

$$\overline{R}^2 = \frac{(\text{Portfolio market risk})^2}{(\text{Portfolio variability})^2}$$

$$= \frac{250}{402}$$

$$= 62 \text{ per cent.}$$

As a portfolio becomes better diversified, the market risk component of total risk increases. In a well-diversified portfolio most of the specific risk is eliminated and thus $\overline{R}^2$ will be close to unity.

The return measures for portfolios are simply the weighted averages of the corresponding returns of the constituent securities. Thus the annual actual return of the portfolio depicted in table 7.2 is calculated as follows, using information from tables 7.1 and 7.2:

$$
\begin{aligned}
\text{Annual actual return of portfolio} &= (0.5)(9) + (0.4)(80) \\
&\quad + (0.1)(-7) \\
&= 36 \text{ per cent.}
\end{aligned}
$$

The quarterly and annual abnormal returns may also be calculated from the data in tables 7.1 and 7.2.

$$
\begin{aligned}
\text{Quarterly abnormal return of portfolio} &= (0.5)(2) + (0.4)(51) \\
&\quad + (0.1)(-9) \\
&= 21 \text{ per cent.}
\end{aligned}
$$

$$
\begin{aligned}
\text{Annual abnormal return of portfolio} &= (0.5)(2) + (0.4)(70) \\
&\quad + (0.1)(-11) \\
&= 28 \text{ per cent.}
\end{aligned}
$$

In this example, the portfolio beta factor, 0.79, is considerably lower than that of the market. Hence, the expected return of the portfolio is also considerably lower than that of the market, since investors are only rewarded for taking on market risk. By contrast, the total risk of the portfolio is 20 per cent, which is equal to the risk of the market portfolio. Clearly, our three-security portfolio is inefficient, since expected return can be increased substantially for the same level of risk by diversification.

The stability of betas

Risk measures are estimated using historical data. In order that betas should be useful as forecasts of future risk levels, it is necessary that they should be stationary over time, or at least only change gradually. If past beta values are to be used in investment decisions, they should provide considerable information about future beta values. Clearly, a company's beta may change because the company itself changes. For example, if a firm's capital structure changes or if the firm changes the nature of its business, this will affect the beta value. Empirical evidence exists regarding the stability of betas for individual shares, unmanaged portfolios of shares, and managed funds.

The general conclusion from studies in both the UK and the USA is that there is some stationarity in the beta factor at the individual security level, but that stationarity improves as stocks are formed into portfolios of increasing size. Widely diversified portfolios tend to have beta values which are very stable over time, and hence these values are extremely useful for forecasting market risk. However, individual securities and poorly diversified portfolios tend to have unstable beta values, which are therefore less reliable for forecasting purposes.

One approach used to investigate the short-run predictability of beta coefficients for individual securities and unmanaged portfolios of securities is to measure betas over successive time-periods and then examine how these betas have changed. For individual securities, the estimates are divided into a number of risk classes on the basis of their ranked beta values, and a transition matrix is then constructed which indicates the movement among risk classes over time. By examining a sequence of pairs of time-periods, an average transition matrix may be calculated. For example, Dimson and Marsh (1982) reported a study for the UK which covered five successive five-year periods from 1955 to 1979 and used five risk classes. The research was based on over 900 shares, and the results indicated that beta estimates for individual shares do show *some* degree of stability over time. In particular, for each initial risk class considered, over 65 per cent of beta estimates fell into the same or an adjacent risk class five years later. For unmanaged portfolios of securities, the betas of individual shares were estimated over a given time-period, and the securities were allocated to one of a group of portfolios on the basis of their ranked betas. The beta of each portfolio was calculated, and then re-estimated using data for the subsequent time-period. The procedure may be repeated over several periods. Dimson and Marsh performed such an analysis on five portfolios, using the same set of data as was used to examine beta stability for individual securities. For each of the four comparisons of two consecutive five-year periods which could be made between 1955 and 1979, the portfolio beta estimates were very stable. In every case, the ranking of the five portfolios according to beta value did not change from the first to the second period.

A second approach used to examine the stationarity of beta coefficients is to calculate the average correlation coefficient between beta estimates made in successive periods. This procedure may be used for individual shares or portfolios of shares. The Dimson and Marsh study showed that the average correlation coefficient between betas in the five adjacent five-year periods from 1955 to 1979 was 0.47 for individual shares. As portfolios of increasing size are considered, the stability of betas increases rapidly. The average correlation coefficient for a portfolio comprising seven shares was 0.82, for a 20-security portfolio 0.93 and for a 100-security portfolio 0.99.

Although the betas of large unmanaged portfolios are highly predictable, this does not imply that the betas of managed funds are also stable. A portfolio manager may deliberately move into low-beta shares prior to an expected market decline, and increase the risk exposure of the fund prior to an expected market upswing. Indeed, a study by Ward and Saunders (1976) showed that the betas of UK unit trusts have varied considerably over time. Therefore, managed funds cannot be relied on to offer a portfolio which exhibits a high level of beta stability.

The betas of individual securities are not particularly stable over time, but the betas of well-diversified unmanaged portfolios are highly predictable. It therefore appears that portfolio management systems which are beta-based are viable for shares traded on the London Stock Exchange, provided that the portfolios comprise a reasonable number of shares.

Portfolio management

Portfolio managers may adopt either an active or a passive management strategy. It is also possible to pursue a combination of active and passive policies.

Passive management accepts all forms of the efficient market hypothesis (EMH). In this case, it is assumed that the stock market is so efficient that it is almost impossible to construct a portfolio which is superior to the market portfolio, and so the equity part of the investor's portfolio should merely comprise the market portfolio. The latter may then be combined with lending or borrowing at the risk-free rate of interest in order to yield, respectively, a (low-risk) lending or (high-risk) borrowing portfolio. The separation theorem discussed in chapter 3 implies that since the market portfolio represents the optimal combination of risky securities, the investor's choice of risk level is a purely financial decision – whether to hold a lending or borrowing portfolio. A passive investment strategy involves constructing and maintaining a portfolio that always lies on the capital market line. The portfolio under management should only be reorganized when there is a change in either the investor's utility function or the market portfolio. A portfolio manager pursuing a passive strategy accepts that it is impossible to beat the market, and thus attempts to minimize transactions and research costs. In practice, the market portfolio may be approximated by index funds. These funds are widely diversified portfolios of securities which attempt to match the performance of broad stock market averages such as the *FT* all-share index.

If the EMH is not entirely accepted, a portfolio manager may engage in active management. This is an attempt to profit from stock selection and/or market timing. A manager who rejects the semi-strong form of the EMH believes that it is possible to use superior analytical skills to construct a portfolio which, if properly managed, will consistently outperform the market portfolio. Such a portfolio manager uses fundamental analysis to identify undervalued securities, which are then used to construct a portfolio with the desired risk level. As the portfolio comprises undervalued securities, it should perform consistently better than the market portfolio. An investment manager who rejects the weak form of the EMH believes that it is possible to beat the market by identifying when a given security or the market is overbought or oversold. This type of portfolio manager uses technical analysis to predict the level of security prices in the immediate future. A comparison of the predicted with the actual price level indicates whether the security (or the market) is currently priced too high or too low.

Combined active–passive management strategies may be used for large portfolios. A proportion of an investment fund may be indexed to the market, and the remainder controlled by active portfolio managers. The higher the degree of confidence in benefiting from active management strategies, the greater the proportion of total assets which will be allocated to active managers.

The *RMS* can assist active portfolio managers in their attempts to outperform the market. With regard to correct market timing, if the investment manager expects the market to move up then the correct strategy is to move into high-β shares. Similarly, if the investment manager expects the market to fall, he should move into low-β shares or go liquid. If the market movement is forecast correctly, the chosen portfolio should outperform the market index. With regard to share selection, the greatest scope for finding undervalued securities occurs among those with the highest specific risk, and thus the *RMS* gives an indication as to where analytical effort should be concentrated. The abnormal return figures for a security show whether it appears to have been undervalued or overvalued in the recent past. If securities are selected which turn out to be undervalued, then the chosen portfolio will outperform the market index.

Further reading

Cohen, J. B., E. D. Zinbarg and A. Zeikel: *Investment Analysis and Portfolio Management*, 5th edn, Homewood, Ill., Richard Irwin, 1987.
Dimson, E., and P. R. Marsh: Modern Risk Measurement. *Managerial Finance*, 5(1), 1979, pp. 80–6.

8
Option pricing theory

Introduction

An option is a contract between two investors, A and B, whereby A pays B a sum of money, and in exchange B grants A the right to buy from or sell to B, at A's discretion, a given asset at a fixed price until a predetermined date, after which any rights or obligations expire. Investor A, who possesses the discretionary right to buy or sell, is known as the buyer of the option or the giver of option money. If he uses his right, investor A is said to exercise or declare the option. Investor B, who grants the right to buy or sell, is called the seller or writer of the option, or the taker of option money. An option to buy is termed a call option, and an option to sell is termed a put option. The sum of money paid for the right of the option is known as the premium or option money. The fixed price specified in the option contract is called the exercise, striking or contract price. The future fixed date is known as the expiration, maturity or last declaration date: a European option may only be exercised on the date when the option expires, whereas an American option may be exercised at any time until the expiration date. Although an option can be based on various types of underlying asset, we shall restrict our attention to the case of an option for quoted ordinary shares.

A call option gives the buyer the right to purchase from the writer, for a specified length of time, a given number of shares in a company at a price fixed by the contract. The benefit to the seller of a call option is that whilst he typically forgoes the opportunity for further appreciation in the value of a stock which he owns, he gains the option premium in the event that the value of the asset drops. The buyer of a call option benefits from being able to control a larger quantity of stock through the payment of option premiums than would be the case if he purchased the stock outright. He gains from any increase in the value of the stock, although his only expenditure is the option premium. His potential loss is limited to the amount of the option money, but this loss will be total unless the share price rises above the exercise price of the option. The option writer has a limited possible gain and potentially unlimited loss. The option buyer has limited possible loss and potentially unlimited gain.

The profit or loss arising from the option contract is illustrated for both seller and buyer in figure 8.1. It is supposed that the exercise price is 100 pence and the option premium is 10 pence. It can be seen that the break-even point is the exercise price plus the option premium; here the option seller and buyer are neither better nor worse off than they would have been if the contract had not been agreed. If the share price at the expiration date is 100 pence or less, the owner of the share gains 10 pence by having written the option, and the option buyer loses 10 pence. As the share price increases from 100 to 110 pence, there is a steady reduction in the option seller's gain and the option buyer's loss. For share prices

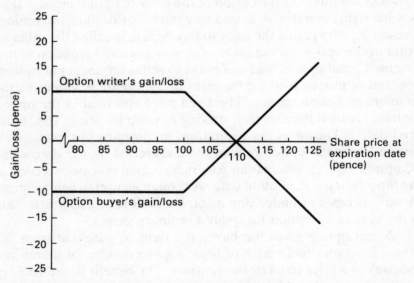

Figure 8.1   Gain/loss arising from call option contract (example)

which exceed 110 pence at the expiration date, the option buyer makes a profit which rises in line with the share price. Similarly, the option writer makes an economic loss for stock prices in excess of 110 pence, since he would have fared better if he had not written the option.

A put option gives the buyer the right of delivering to the writer, for a specified length of time, a given number of shares in a company at a price fixed by the contract. The positions of the option buyer and option writer in the case of the put contract are reversed compared with those obtaining under the call contract; for a put option, the writer gains from any increase in the value of the stock and the buyer benefits if the share price falls.

By far the most popular type of option contract is the call option, and so in our subsequent discussion we shall concentrate on this type of contract. Furthermore, for simplifying purposes we shall assume that options are European, so they may only be exercised on the expiration date, and that no cash payments are made by the underlying asset.

Option markets

Traditional (or *conventional*) options have been available for some considerable time, but *traded* (or *listed*) options only appeared for the first time in 1973 with the opening of the Chicago Board Option Exchange. Organized markets for options were established subsequently in several major financial centres of the world, and, since 1978, include the London Traded Option Market (LTOM), to which our discussion of traded options relates.

Prior to 1973, it was only possible to buy and sell options on an *ad hoc* basis through an option dealer. Hence the expiration date, exercise price and option price had to be negotiated for each individual contract, which led to lack of uniformity among contracts and high transaction costs. In addition, the problem existed of how to guarantee a contract against default. Also, in general, once an option had been created it could only be exercised or allowed to expire, since there was no significant secondary market for unexpired options. As a result of these problems, little business was done in traditional options.

With traded options, the link between option buyer and option writer is broken by the use of a central clearing system. Here trading is facilitated by the use of contracts with uniform terms, and relatively low transaction costs compared with traditional options. The set of all call options (or all put options) on the shares of a given company is termed a class of exchange traded options. The maximum life of an option is nine months, and there are only four potential expiration dates for a particular class of options. When a new class is introduced, the options are allocated permanently to a quarterly cycle of either January, April, July and October, or February, May, August and November.

The London Options Clearing House (LOCH), a company owned by the London Stock Exchange, is responsible for the settlement of all traded option transactions. Appropriate collateral is given by the option writer to the LOCH to guarantee that the contract will be fulfilled should the option be exercised. Hence the option buyer is protected from the risk of default by the option writer.

An alternative to exercising an option is to sell it. By making a closing sale, the holder of a LOCH option disposes of it in the market. Also, the writer of a LOCH option may make a closing purchase by buying an option identical to the one he has written, in order to extinguish his liability. In practice, only 5 to 10 per cent of traded options are exercised, as generally options either expire worthless or closing sales and purchases are executed.

Factors affecting the price of an option

The market price of an option (or option premium) is determined by the following set of factors:

1 The current price of the underlying share.
2 The exercise price.
3 The length of time to expiration.
4 The risk attaching to the underlying share.
5 The risk-free rate of interest.

Obviously, we should expect that the higher the current market value of a share, the greater the value of an option written on it, *ceteris paribus*. Similarly, the lower the exercise price, the higher the value of the option. Now the minimum possible level of the option premium is termed the intrinsic value of the option. If the current price of the underlying share exceeds the exercise price – that is, the option is 'in the money' – then the intrinsic value of the option is the difference between the share price and exercise price. If the exercise price exceeds the current share price – that is, the option is 'out of the money' – then the intrinsic value of the option is zero. The intrinsic value thus depends merely on the share price and exercise price.

The excess of the option premium over its intrinsic value is known as the time value of the option. For example, even if the share price is less than the exercise price, the option will still be valuable provided that investors believe that there is a chance that the share price will exceed the exercise price before the option expires. On account of the possibility that the share price may be at a higher level in the future than now, investors are generally prepared to pay more for an option than its intrinsic value; that is, the time value of an option is positive. The greater the length of time to maturity, the higher the time value of the option, since there is increasing opportunity for the price of the underlying share to rise. Thus the value of an option increases with the length of time to expiration.

The price of an option varies with the risk of the underlying share. Clearly, if there were no risk (that is, the variance of the return of the share were zero) then the price of the share would remain constant into the future, and the time value of the option would be zero. The more risky the underlying share, the more valuable the option, as there is a higher probability that the share price will exceed the exercise price, and the option holder only benefits if this latter condition obtains at the expiration date. For a given expected return, the investor prefers to hold shares with minimum risk but options on shares which have maximum risk.

The risk-free rate of interest also affects the value of an option. By purchasing an option, the holder is provided with a form of gearing. If an investor expects the price of a share to rise in the future, he may purchase either the share itself or an option on that share in order to realize the expected capital gain. If the current price of the underlying share is 200 pence and the option price is 20 pence, then the holder spends 180 pence less by buying the option rather than the share. An option thus provides a substitute for borrowing. The higher the risk-free rate of interest, the greater the amount of interest saved by purchasing the option rather than the share, and therefore the higher the value of the option.

The market value of an option is given by the following relationship:

$$P_o = f(P_s, E, \sigma, T, R_F) \tag{8.1}$$

where P_o is the current value of the option, P_s is the current price of the share, E is the exercise price of the option, σ is the standard deviation of the return of the share, T is the length of time to expiration of the option, R_F is the risk-free rate of interest, and f is some function.

The partial derivatives of the option price with respect to the various arguments are

$$\frac{\partial P_o}{\partial P_s} > 0, \ \frac{\partial P_o}{\partial E} < 0, \ \frac{\partial P_o}{\partial \sigma} > 0, \ \frac{\partial P_o}{\partial T} > 0, \ \frac{\partial P_o}{\partial R_F} > 0. \tag{8.2}$$

The Black–Scholes option valuation formula

Black and Scholes (1973) have derived a formula for the valuation of options. Their main assumptions, in addition to our previous simplifications – that only European call options are being considered, and that no cash payments are made by the underlying asset – are that there are no taxes or transaction costs, and that the underlying stock's continuously compounded return follows a normal distribution with a constant variance (so the expiration price is lognormally distributed).

The Black–Scholes model is based on the idea that it is possible for investors in the underlying stock to hedge their positions – that is, owners of the stock can write call options on that stock. Indeed, investors can set up a perfectly hedged position comprising a long position in the underlying stock and a short position in options written on that stock. This perfectly hedged portfolio is risk-free and therefore should earn the risk-free rate of interest in equilibrium, on the assumption that capital markets are efficient. As the share price changes over time, the number of options which must be sold short in order to create a hedged position with a share alters. In order to maintain the risk-free hedge, it is necessary continuously to readjust the ratio of shares to options in the portfolio. Now the option premium at which the perfectly hedged position yields the risk-free rate of interest is the fair value of the option.

Black and Scholes use the mathematical technique of stochastic calculus to derive the following formula for the valuation of an option:

$$P_o = P_s N(d_1) - \frac{E}{e^{R_F T}} N(d_2) \tag{8.3}$$

where

$$d_1 = \frac{\ln(P_s/E) + (R_F + \frac{1}{2}\sigma^2)T}{\sigma\sqrt{T}}$$

$$d_2 = \frac{\ln(P_s/E) + (R_F - \frac{1}{2}\sigma^2)T}{\sigma\sqrt{T}}$$

and where P_o, P_s and E are as defined previously, σ is the standard deviation of the continuously compounded annual rate of return of the share, T is the length of time to expiration of the option (in years), R_F is the continuously compounded risk-free rate of interest, e = 2.71828, ln denotes natural logarithm, and $N(d)$ is the probability that a deviation less than d will occur in a normal distribution with mean equal to zero and standard deviation equal to 1.

If one takes the partial derivatives of the option price, it can be seen that the latter is an increasing function of the share price, the riskiness of the share, the time to expiration and the risk-free rate of interest, and a decreasing function of the exercise price, thus satisfying the conditions imposed by inequalities (8.2).

In order to use equation (8.3) to value an option, data are required on the share price, exercise price, time to maturity, risk-free rate of interest and the standard deviation of the rate of return of the share. Share price information is readily available, and the exercise price and time to maturity are given for each option. The risk-free rate of interest may easily be approximated. The riskiness of the underlying share is usually obtained from historical data; for example, the London Business School's *Risk Measurement Service* provides estimates of the variabilities (or standard deviations) of return for all tabulated shares. The only additional requirement in order to perform the calculations implied by the option valuation formula (8.3) is that logarithm tables and cumulative normal distribution tables should be available.

The Black–Scholes option pricing formula was derived under a fairly restrictive set of assumptions. For example, dividend payments on the underlying stock were not permitted, and the transaction costs of maintaining a hedged position were not allowed for. Amendments to the Black–Scholes model have therefore been proposed to correct for these flaws (see, for example, Gastineau (1988), chapter 7). The resulting models are, of course, far more complex. Furthermore, empirical tests of the Black–Scholes model indicate that it seems to fit reality reasonably well. Empirical evidence from the USA reported by Black and Scholes (1972) – for traditional options – and Galai (1977) – for traded options – implies that the Black–Scholes option pricing model predicts prices so well that it is possible to earn excess returns in the absence of transaction costs. These excess returns disappear, however, once transaction costs are introduced, so prices are determined efficiently down to the level of transaction costs.

Implications of option pricing theory for corporate financial policy

Option pricing theory has numerous implications for corporate financial policy. For example, the equity in a levered firm may be viewed as a call option on the value of the firm's assets. When shareholders issue bonds, this is equivalent to selling the firm's assets to the bondholders in exchange for cash and a call option. The exercise price is the set of payments promised to the debt holders. If the value of the firm is less than the exercise price (that is, in the event of bankruptcy), shareholders will not exercise their option and the firm's assets will be retained by the bondholders. If the value of the firm exceeds the exercise price, shareholders will exercise their option by making the payments promised to the bondholders, and thus re-acquire the firm's assets. It is the shareholders' ability to declare bankruptcy which gives a share the attributes of a call option, and the importance of these characteristics will depend upon the degree to which the firm is levered and the probability of bankruptcy.

Option pricing theory has many other applications in the area of corporate finance. It yields implications for the firm's capital structure and dividend policy, and also for mergers and acquisitions. Galai and Masulis (1976) show how the theory may be applied to such issues in corporate finance. Option pricing theory is relatively new, and it is being applied to more and more concepts. Insurance, house mortgages, warrants, convertible bonds, and so on, may all be thought of as options. For the portfolio manager, we suggest that although options are new and unfamiliar, they do offer a vehicle for exploitation of inside information and forecasting ability, and a mechanism for adjusting portfolio risk.

Further reading

Black, F., and M. Scholes: The Pricing of Options and Corporate Liabilities. *Journal of Political Economy*, 81(3), May–June 1973, pp. 637–54.

Bealey, R., and S. Myers: *Principles of Corporate Finance*, New York, McGraw-Hill, 1991, chapter 21.

Copeland, T. E., and J. F. Weston: *Financial Theory and Corporate Policy*, London, Addison-Wesley, 1988, chapter 8.

Elton, E. J., and M. J. Gruber: *Modern Portfolio Theory and Investment Analysis*, 4th edn, New York, John Wiley, 1991, chapter 20.

Hull, J. C.: *Options Futures and Other Derivative Securities*, Englewood Cliffs, NJ, Prentice Hall, 1989.

9
Concluding comments

We have now completed our review of portfolio theory and investment management. In the previous edition of this book, published in 1983, we reached what at first glance seemed to be a sad conclusion – that stock markets were efficient and that it was very difficult for any investor to achieve excess returns. How far does the research over the last ten years alter our conclusions? The discovery of excess volatility and numerous anomalies seems to suggest trading strategies which may lead to excess returns. But can investors easily capitalize on these strategies and are anomalies likely to recur? We believe that this is an open question, so we leave it for the reader to make up his or her own mind. What does seem to be clear is that it is unlikely in such a competitive market that gains can be made easily. However, modern portfolio theory does offer a rational approach to investment management, whereby rewards are generally commensurate with the level of accepted market risk. Passive management must be recommended for the vast majority of investors. Obvious inefficiencies such as taxation should be considered by all investors. All portfolio managers should determine the level of risk appropriate to the portfolio, minimize transaction costs, and regularly review the level of portfolio risk. For those market activists with luck, inside information, or the capacity to discover inefficiency by developing forecasting ability, risk measurement services provide the necessary data to assist in beating the market.

Appendix:
study questions

Chapter 1

1 Explain the following five important ideas in modern portfolio theory (MPT):
  (a) Return
  (b) Risk
  (c) Risk versus return
  (d) Diversification
  (e) The efficient market hypothesis.

2 Prepare transparencies illustrating:
  (a) The characteristic line
  (b) The capital market line
  (c) The security market line.
  Explain them to your group members.

3 Discuss the following:
  (a) The market model
  (b) The capital asset pricing model.

4 Prepare a transparency showing how diversification reduces risk.
  Explain:
  (a) Total risk
  (b) Specific risk
  (c) Market risk.

5 Discuss developments in MPT since World War II.

Chapter 2

1 Prepare a transparency illustrating the Markowitz mean-variance approach to portfolio management. Explain:
   (a) Mean
   (b) Variance and standard deviation
   (c) Attainable portfolio
   (d) Efficient set
   (e) Utility curves.

2 Assess the Markowitz contribution to MPT.

3 How can investors reduce risk by international diversification?

4 The securities of companies A, B and C have the following expected returns, variances of return and covariances of return:

Expected returns:	Company	Expected return (%)
	A	7
	B	10
	C	14

Variance–covariance matrix:		Company		
		A	B	C
	Company A	400	200	300
	B	200	700	100
	C	300	100	1000

Calculate the expected return and standard deviation of return for a portfolio in which the securities of companies A, B and C are held in proportions 0.5, 0.4 and 0.1 respectively.

5 The securities of companies A and B have the following expected returns and standard deviations of return:

Company	Expected return (%)	Standard deviation of return (%)
A	12	17
B	9	14

In addition, the expected correlation of returns between the two stocks is 0.6.

(a) Calculate the expected return and risk for the following portfolios:
    (i) 100% in A
    (ii) 100% in B
    (iii) 75% in A, 25% in B
    (iv) 25% in A, 75% in B
    (v) 50% in A, 50% in B.

(b) How much of the portfolio should be invested in company A in order to minimize risk?
(c) Plot the results.
(d) Which of the portfolios described in (a) and (b) are optional?
(e) Repeat (a), (b), (c) and (d) for expected correlations of:
    (i) −0.6
    (ii) 1.0
    (iii) −1.0
    (iv) 0.0.

Chapter 3

1 Prepare a transparency illustrating the capital market line. Explain:
   (a) The zero-beta portfolio
   (b) The all-equity portfolio with no specific risk
   (c) Leveraged portfolios
   (d) Lending portfolios.

2 Discuss the validity of the CAPM and examine its value in assessing portfolio performance.

3 Suppose that the risk-free rate of interest is 7%, and the market portfolio has an expected return of 15% and a standard deviation of return of 18%. Calculate the expected return for a portfolio with no specific risk and a standard deviation of return of 22%.

4 What is the beta of an efficient portfolio with an expected return of 12% if the risk-free rate of interest is 6% and the market portfolio has an expected return of 16% and a standard deviation of return of 20%? What is the risk of the portfolio?

5 Assume that the risk-free rate of interest is 8% and the market portfolio has an expected return of 18%. Calculate the expected return for a security with a beta value of:
   (a) 0.0
   (b) 0.5

(c) 1.0

(d) 2.0.

6 Suppose that the expected return of a security is 10%, the risk-free rate of interest is 6% and the expected market risk premium is 7%. What will be the expected return of the security if its market sensitivity doubles?

7 Suppose that, over a five-year period, the average risk-free rate of interest was 7%, the average market return was 12% and the performances of four portfolio managers were as follows:

Portfolio manager	Average return (%)	Beta
A	10	0.70
B	12	0.95
C	13	1.20
D	16	1.35

(a) Calculate the expected return for each portfolio manager.

(b) Calculate the risk-adjusted excess return for each portfolio manager.

(c) Rank the portfolio managers in terms of risk-adjusted performance.

Chapter 4

1 Prepare transparencies illustrating any three of the weak form tests of the efficient market hypothesis. Explain to your group members.

2 Prepare transparencies illustrating any three of the semi-strong form tests of the efficient market hypothesis. Explain to your group members.

3 Prepare transparencies illustrating any three of the strong form tests of the efficient market hypothesis. Explain to your group members.

Chapter 5

1 Prepare transparencies illustrating the techniques available to technical analysts. Explain their value to your group members.

2 Prepare transparencies illustrating the techniques available to fundamental analysts. Explain their value to your group members.

3 Show:

(a) The mathematical 'proof' of dividend irrelevance

(b) The graphical 'proof' of dividend irrelevance.

Explain their applicability to the 'real' world.

4 On joining a firm of merchant bankers, you are asked to make a 30-minute presentation to some of the firm's clients entitled 'Investment Management in Perfectly Efficient Markets'. Prepare your presentation assuming that your audience will include widows, gamblers, executors and pension fund managers.

5 How might the individual investor attempt to exploit market inefficiencies?

6 (a) A City editor recently informed readers that small investors are getting out of the market because they cannot compete with the aids available to professional portfolio managers – computers and financial expertise. Comment.

 (b) Last week a company's earnings were announced. They were down 30% on the previous year, the dividend being cut by 40%. The share price rose 40p. Why?

 (c) My bank manager tells me that the best long-term investment is the bank's unit trusts. Why? Will they come up with the goods?

 (d) The best system for making money in stocks and shares is to get rid of anything that falls 5% and hold on to other investments until they make 50%. Comment.

 (e) A merchant bank recently advised a private company not to go public until early summer, by which time the *FT* index should be through the 1,000 barrier. Is this good advice?

Chapter 6

1 Consider the anomalies discussed in the first part of the chapter. Which are the most economically significant and which are most likely to lead to profitable trading rules? What factors, if any, do you consider likely to hinder exploitation of these anomalies?

2 Explain the evidence which suggests that individuals frequently do not make rational decisions? Why do some financial economists doubt whether the experimental results of psychologists can be replicated in the real world?

3 Describe the intuition behind the volatility tests conducted by Shiller. If the market really exhibits more volatility than can be attributed to changes in fundamentals, why may it be difficult for investors to capitalize on this excess volatility and make excess returns?

4 Some authors have suggested that fashions and fads may influence stock prices. Do you find the arguments convincing? What evidence, if any, supports the idea that fashions and fads have an impact on stock prices, and what evidence tends to refute this?

Chapter 7

1 Prepare transparencies showing how an investor with forecasting ability can use the *RMS* to achieve excess returns on:
(a) A single security
(b) The market.

2 Present statistics relating to three companies from the *RMS*. Explain the differences to your group members.

3 Interpret and comment on each of the tabulated figures in table A1.

4 Suppose that you have invested 50 per cent of your money in the Avon Rubber Co. Ltd, 30 per cent in Babcock International and 20 per cent in the Bank of Scotland stk. Use the data provided in question 3 to analyse the risk and performance of your portfolio. Is your portfolio well diversified?

Chapter 8

1 A property is on the market for £100,000. You are considering offering the owner £10,000 for the option to buy the property for £95,000. Explain how the £10,000 option price would be affected by:
(a) A change in the property's value
(b) A change in the offer price
(c) The duration of the option
(d) The volatility of the property's market value
(e) Interest rates.

2 Prepare transparencies illustrating the value of a European call option. Explain to your group members.

3 Present data from the *Financial Times* illustrating the prices of call and put options. Explain to your group members.

4 Explain the possible relevance of OPT for:
(a) Debt–equity decisions
(b) The valuation of warrants
(c) Adjustment of portfolio risk
(d) Exploitation of inside information.

5 Calculate the value of a three-month European call option with an exercise price of £20 if the current share price is £17, the standard deviation of the continuously compounded annual rate of return of the

Table A1

Company name	Stock exchange industry classification	Variability (%)	Beta	Specific risk (%)	Standard error	R^2 (%)	Annual actual return (%)	Quarterly abnormal return (%)	Annual abnormal return (%)
Avon Rubber Co. Ltd	Motor components	40	0.9	37	0.18	16	−5	5	−36
Babcock International	Miscellaneous mechanical engineering	35	1.21	28	0.16	37	67	40	29
Bank of Scotland stk	Banks	25	0.72	22	0.13	26	11	−10	−16

The above data appear in the *Risk Measurement Service*, April 1983.

share is 0.6 and the risk-free rate of interest is 7%. No dividends are expected to be declared over the next three months.

6 What is the maximum price you would be willing to pay to purchase a European call option with an exercise price of £15 and expiring in 100 days, if the current share price is £20? Assume that the continuously compounded annual rate of return variance of the share is 0.7 and the risk-free rate of interest is 8%.

References

Alexander, S. S., 1961: Price movements in speculative markets: trends or random walks. *Industrial Management Review*, 2, May, pp. 7–26.

Ambachtsheer, K., 1974: Profit potential in an 'almost efficient' market. *Journal of Portfolio Management*, 1(1), Fall pp. 84–7.

Ammer, J. M., 1990: *Expenses, yields and excess returns: New evidence on closed end fund discounts from the UK*, London, London School of Economics, Discussion Paper 108.

Ariel, R. A., 1987: A monthly effect in stock returns. *Journal of Financial Economics*, 18(1), pp. 161–74.

Bachelier, L., 1900: Théorie de la spéculation. In P. H. Cootner (ed.): *The Random Character of Stock Market Prices*, Cambridge, Mass., MIT Press, 1964, pp. 17–78.

Ball, R., and J. Bowers, 1988: Daily seasonals in equity and fixed interest returns: Australian evidence and tests of plausible hypotheses. In E. Dimson (ed.), *Stockmarket Anomalies*, Cambridge, Cambridge University Press, pp. 74–90.

Ball, R., and P. Brown, 1968: An empirical evaluation of accounting income numbers. *Journal of Accounting Research*, Autumn, pp. 159–78.

Banz, R. W., 1981: The relationship between return and market value of common stocks. *Journal of Financial Economics*, 9, p. 3–18.

Basu, S., 1977: Investment performance of common stocks in relation to their price–earnings ratios: A test of the efficient market hypothesis. *Journal of Finance*, 32(3), June, pp. 663–82.

Baumol, W. J., 1963: An expected gain-confidence limit criterion for portfolio selection. *Management Science*, 9, October, pp. 174–82.

Berges, A., J. J. McConnell and G. G. Schlarbaum, 1984: Turn of the year in Canada. *Journal of Finance*, 39, March, pp. 185–92.

Black, F., 1986: Noise. *Journal of Finance*, 41(3), July, pp. 529–43.

Black, F., and M. Scholes, 1972: The valuation of option contracts and a test of market efficiency. *Journal of Finance*, 27, May, pp. 399–417.

Black, F., and M. Scholes, 1973: The pricing of options and corporate liabilities. *Journal of Political Economy*, 81(3), May–June, pp. 637–54.

Blume, M., and I. Friend, 1973: A new look at the capital asset pricing model. *Journal of Finance*, 28, March, pp. 19–33.

Blume, M., and R. Stambaugh, 1983: Biases in computed returns: An application to the size effect. *Journal of Financial Economics*, 12, pp. 387–404.

Brealey, R. A., and S. Myers, 1991: *The Principles of Corporate Finance*, New York, McGraw-Hill.

Breeden, D. T., 1979: An inter-temporal asset pricing model with stochastic consumption and investment opportunities. *Journal of Financial Economics*, 7, pp. 265–96.

Brown, P., D. Keim, A. Kleidon and T. Marsh, 1983: Stock return seasonality and the tax-loss selling hypothesis: Analysis of arguments and Australian evidence. *Journal of Financial Economics*, 12(1), pp. 105–28.

Brown, P., A. Kleidon and T. Marsh, 1983: New evidence on the nature of size-related anomalies in stock prices. *Journal of Financial Economics*, 12, pp. 33–56.

Bulkley, G., and I. Tonks, 1989: Are UK stock prices excessively volatile? Trading rules and variance bounds tests. *Economic Journal*, 99, pp. 1083–98.

Cecchetti, S. G., P. Lam and N. Mark, 1990: Mean reversion in equilibrium asset prices. *American Economic Review*, 80(3), June, pp. 398–418.

Chen, Nai-Fu, R. Roll and S. Ross, 1986: Economic forces and the stock market. *Journal of Business*, 59(3), July, pp. 383–403.

Cochrane, J. H., 1991: Volatility tests and efficient markets: A review essay. *Journal of Monetary Economics*, 27(3), June, pp. 463–86.

Cohen, K. J., and G. A. Pogue, 1967: An empirical evaluation of alternative portfolio selection models. *Journal of Business*, 40, April, pp. 166–93.

Cootner, P. H., 1962: Stock prices: random vs systematic changes. *Industrial Management Review*, 3, Spring, pp. 24–45.

Copeland, T. E., and J. F. Weston, 1988: *Financial Theory and Corporate Policy*, 3rd edn, Reading, Mass., Addison-Wesley.

Corhay, A., G. Hawawini and P. Michel, 1988: The pricing of equity on the London Stock Exchange: seasonality and size premium. In E. Dimson (ed.), *Stock Market Anomalies*, Cambridge, Cambridge University Press, pp. 197–212.

Cross, F., 1973: The behaviour of stock prices on Fridays and Mondays. *Financial Analysts Journal*, 29(6), November–December, pp. 67–79.

Cunningham, S. W., 1973: The predictability of British stock market prices. *Applied Statistics*, 22(3), pp. 315–31.

De Bondt, W. F., and R. Thaler, 1985: Does the stock market overreact? *Journal of Finance*, 40(3), July, pp. 793–805.

Dimson, E., and P. Marsh, 1979: Modern risk measurement. *Managerial Finance*, 5(1), pp. 80–6.

Dimson, E., and P. Marsh (eds), 1982: *Risk Measurement Service*, 4(3), July, pp. 2–12.

Dimson, E., and P. Marsh, 1984: An analysis of brokers' and analysts' unpublished forecasts of UK stock returns. *Journal of Finance*, 39(5), December, pp. 1257–92.

Dimson, E., S. Hodges and P. R. Marsh, 1980: International diversification. Paper presented at seminar on 'The coming revolution in investment management', London Business School, January.

Fama, E. F., 1965: The behaviour of stock prices. *Journal of Business*, 38, January, pp. 34–105.

Fama, E. F., M. Fisher, M. Jensen and R. Roll, 1969: The adjustment of stock prices to new information. *International Economic Review*, 10(1), February, pp. 1–21.

Fama, E. F., and K. R. French, 1988a: Permanent and temporary components of stock prices. *Journal of Political Economy*, 96(2), April, pp. 246–73.

Fama, E. F., and K. R. French, 1988b: Dividend yields and expected stock returns. *Journal of Financial Economics*, 22, pp. 3–25.

Fama, E. F., and K. R. French, 1989: Business conditions and expected returns on stocks and bonds. *Journal of Financial Economics*, 25, pp. 23–49.

Fama, E. F., and J. D. MacBeth, 1973: Risk, return and equilibrium: empirical tests. *Journal of Political Economy*, 81(3), May–June, pp. 607–36.

Firth, M., 1978: *Unit Trusts: Performance and Prospects*, Bradford, MCB Publications.

Flavin, M. A., 1983: Excess volatility in financial markets: A re-assessment of the empirical evidence. *Journal of Political Economy*, 91(6), December, pp. 929–56.

Francis, J. C., 1991: *Investments: Analysis and Management*, 5th edn, New York, McGraw-Hill.

French, K., 1980: Stock returns and the weekend effect. *Journal of Financial Economics*, 8(1), pp. 55–69.

French, K., and R. W. Roll, 1986: Stock return variances: The arrival of information and the reaction of traders. *Journal of Financial Economics*, 17(1), pp. 5–26.

Friend, I., M. Blume and J. Crockett, 1970: *Mutual Funds and Other Institutional Investors: A New Perspective*, New York, McGraw-Hill.

Friend, I., F. Brown, E. Herman and D. Vickers, 1962: *A Study of Mutual Funds* (The Wharton Report), Washington, US Government Printing Office.

Galai, D., 1977: Tests of market efficiency of the Chicago Board Options Exchange. *Journal of Business*, 50(2), April, pp. 167–97.

Galai, D., and R. W. Masulis, 1976: The option pricing model and the risk factor of stock. *Journal of Financial Economics*, 3, p. 53.

Gastineau, G. L., 1988: *The Stock Options Manual*, 3rd edn, New York, McGraw-Hill.

Gibbons, M., and P. Hess, 1981: Day of the week effects and asset returns. *Journal of Business*, 54, October, pp. 579–96.

Granger, C., and O. Morgenstern, 1963: Spectral analysis of New York stock market prices. *Kyklos*, 16, pp. 1–27.

Grether, D. M., and C. R. Plott, 1979: Economic theory of choice and the preference reversal phenomenon. *American Economic Review*, 69, September, pp. 623–38.

Grubel, H. G., 1968: Internationally diversified portfolios: welfare gains and capital flows. *American Economic Review*, 58, December, pp. 1299–314.

Gultekin, M. N., and N. B. Gultekin, 1983: Stock market seasonality: International evidence. *Journal of Financial Economics*, 12(4), pp. 469–82.

Gultekin, M. N., and N. B. Gultekin, 1987: Stock return anomalies and tests of the APT. *Journal of Finance*, 42(5), December, 1213–24.

Harris, L., 1986: A transaction data study of weekly and intra daily patterns in stock returns. *Journal of Financial Economics*, 16(1), pp. 99–117.

Her Majesty's Stationery Office, *Business Monitor*, various issues.

Jaffe, J., 1974: The effect of regulation changes on insider trading. *The Bell Journal of Economics and Management Science*, Spring, pp. 93–121.

Jaffe, J., and R. Westerfield, 1985: The week end effect in common stock returns: The international evidence. *Journal of Finance*, 40(2), June, pp. 433–54.

Jensen, M. C., 1968: The performance of mutual funds in the period 1945–64. *Journal of Finance*, 23, May, pp. 389–416.

Jensen, M. C., 1972: Capital markets: theory and evidence. *Bell Journal of Economics and Management Science*, Autumn, pp. 357–98.

Jensen, M. C., 1978: Symposium on some anomalous evidence regarding market efficiency. *Journal of Financial Economics*, 6, p. 95.

Jensen, M. C., and M. Scholes, 1972: The capital asset pricing model: some empirical tests. In M. C. Jensen (ed.), *Studies in the Theory of Capital Markets*, New York, Praeger.

Kahneman, D., and A. Tversky, 1973: On the psychology of prediction. *Psychological Review*, 80(4), pp. 237–51.

Kaplan, R. S., and R. Roll, 1972: Investor evaluation of accounting information: some empirical evidence. *Journal of Business*, 45, April, pp. 225–57.

Keim, D. B., 1983: Size related anomalies and stock market seasonality: Further empirical evidence. *Journal of Financial Economics*, 12, pp. 13–32.

Keim, D. B., and R. F. Stambaugh, 1984: A further investigation of the weekend effect in stock returns. *Journal of Finance*, 39(3), July, pp. 819–37.

Kendall, M. G., 1953: The analysis of economic time-series. *Journal of the Royal Statistical Society*, 96(1), pp. 11–25.

Keynes, J. M., 1936: *The General Theory of Employment, Interest and Money*, New York, Harcourt Brace.

Kim, Myung Jig, C. R. Nelson and R. Startz, 1991: Mean reversion in stock prices? A reappraisal of the empirical evidence. *Review of Economic Studies*, 58, pp. 515–28.

Kleidon, A. W., 1986: Variance bounds tests and stock price valuation models. *Journal of Political Economy*, 94(5), October, pp. 953–1001.

Kraus, A., and H. Stoll, 1972: Price impacts of block trading on the New York stock exchange. *Journal of Finance*, 27(3), June, pp. 569–88.

Lakonishok, J., and M. Levi, 1982: Weekend effects on stock returns: A note. *Journal of Finance*, 37(3), June, pp. 883–9.

Lakonishok, J., and S. Smidt, 1988: Are seasonal anomalies real? A ninety year perspective. *Review of Financial Studies*, 1(4), Winter, pp. 403–25.

Le Roy, S. F., and R. Porter, 1981: The present-value relation: Tests based on implied variance bounds. *Econometrica*, 49(3), May, pp. 555–74.

Lee, C. M., A. Shleifer and R. Thaler, 1991: Investor sentiment and the closed end fund puzzle. *Journal of Finance*, 46(1), March, pp. 75–109.

Levis, M., 1989: Stock market anomalies: A re-assessment based on UK evidence. *Journal of Banking and Finance* 13(4–5), September, pp. 675–96.

Levis, M., and D. Thomas, 1992: *Initial public offerings of investment trusts*, London, City University Business School, Working Paper.

Levy, H., and M. Sarnat, 1970: International diversification of investment portfolios. *American Economic Review*, 60, September, pp. 668–75.

Lichenstein, S., and P. Slovic, 1971: Reversals of preference between bids and choices in gambling decisions: *Journal of Experimental Psychology*, 89, January, pp. 46–55.

Lichenstein, S., and P. Slovic, 1973: Response-induced reversals and preference in gambling: An extended replication in Las Vegas. *Journal of Experimental Psychology*, 101, November, pp. 16–20.

Lintner, J., 1965: The valuation of risky assets and the selection of risky investments in stock portfolios and capital budgets. *Review of Econ-*

omics and Statistics, 47, February, pp. 13–37.

Mandelbrot, B., 1963: The variation of certain speculative prices. *Journal of Business*, 36, October, pp. 394–419.

Mandelker, G., 1974: Risk and return: the case of merging firms. *Journal of Financial Economics*, 1, p. 303.

Markowitz, H. M., 1952: Portfolio selection. *Journal of Finance*, 7, March, pp. 77–91.

Markowitz, H. M., 1959: *Portfolio Selection: Efficient Diversification of Investment*, New York, Wiley.

Marsh, P. R., 1980: Measuring risk. Unpublished paper, London Business School.

Marsh, T., and R. C. Merton, 1986: Dividend variability and variance bounds tests for the rationality of stock market prices. *American Economic Review*, 76(3), June, pp. 483–98.

Mayers, D., and E. Rice, 1978: Measuring portfolio performance and the empirical content of asset pricing models. *Journal of Financial Economics*, 7(1), pp. 3–28.

McNeil, B. J., S. G. Pauker, H. C. Sox and A. Tversky, 1982: On the elicitation of preferences for alternative therapies. *New England Journal of Medicine*, 306, pp. 1259–62.

Merton, R. C., 1987: On the current state of the stock market rationality hypothesis. In S. Fischer et al. (eds): *Macroeconomics and Finance: Essays in honor of Franco Modigliani*, Cambridge, Mass., MIT Press, pp. 93–124.

Moore, A., 1964: Some characteristics of changes in common stock prices. In P. Cootner (ed.): *The Random Character of Stock Market Prices*, Cambridge, Mass., MIT Press.

Nakamura, T., and N. Terada, 1984: The size effect and seasonality in Japanese stock returns. Manuscript, Nomura Research Institute, London.

Newbould, G. D., and P. S. Poon, 1993: The minimum number of stocks needed for diversification. *Financial Practice and Education*, Fall.

Niederhoffer, F. M., and M. F. M. Osborne, 1966: Market making and reversal on the stock exchange. *Journal of the American Statistical Association*, 61, December, pp. 897–916.

Osborne, M. F. M., 1959: Brownian motion in the stock market. *Operations Research*, March–April, pp. 145–73.

Pettit, R. R., 1972: Dividend announcements, security performance and capital market efficiency. *Journal of Finance*, 25(5), December, pp. 993–1007.

Poon, S., and S. J. Taylor, 1991: Macroeconomic factors and the UK stock market. *Journal of Business Finance and Accounting*, 18(5), September, pp. 619–36.

Poterba, J., and L. Summers, 1988: Mean reversion in stock prices:

Evidence and implications. *Journal of Financial Economics*, 22, pp. 27–59.

Reinganum, M. R., 1981: Abnormal returns in small firms' portfolios. *Financial Analysts Journal*, 37, March–April, pp. 52–7.

Reinganum, M. R., 1982: A direct test of Roll's conjecture on the firm size effect. *Journal of Finance*, 37(1), March, pp. 27–35.

Roberts, H. V., 1959: Stock market 'patterns' and financial analysis: methodological suggestions. *Journal of Finance*, 14, March, pp. 1–10.

Roll, R., 1977: A critique of the asset pricing theory's tests: Part I: on past and potential testability of the theory. *Journal of Financial Economics*, 4, pp. 129–76.

Roll, R., 1980: Performance evaluation and benchmark errors (I). *Journal of Portfolio Management*, 6(4), Summer, pp. 5–12.

Roll, R., 1983: Vas ist das? The turn of the year effect and return premium of small firms. *Journal of Portfolio Management*, 9(1), Winter, pp. 18–28.

Roll, R., and S. Ross, 1980: An empirical investigation of the arbitrage pricing theory. *Journal of Finance*, 35(5), December, pp. 1073–103.

Rosenberg, B., K. Reid and R. Lanstein, 1985: Persuasive evidence of market inefficiency. *Journal of Portfolio Management*, 11(3), Spring, pp. 9–16.

Ross, S., 1976: The arbitrage theory of capital asset pricing. *Journal of Economic Theory*, December, pp. 343–62.

Rozeff, M. S., and W. R. Kinney, 1976: Capital market seasonality: The case of stock returns. *Journal of Financial Economics*, 3, pp. 379–402.

Ryan, T. M., 1978: *Theory of Portfolio Selection*, London, Macmillan.

Samuelson, P. A., 1965: Proof that properly anticipated prices fluctuate randomly. *Industrial Management Review*, 6, Spring, pp. 41–9.

Scholes, M., 1972: The market for securities: Substitution versus price pressure and the effects of information on share prices. *Journal of Business*, 45(2), April, pp. 179–211.

Sharpe, W. F., 1963: A simplified model for portfolio analysis. *Management Science*, 9(2), January, pp. 277–93.

Sharpe, W. F., 1964: Capital asset prices: A theory of market equilibrium under conditions of risk. *Journal of Finance*, 19, September, pp. 425–42.

Sharpe, W. F., 1966: Mutual fund performance. *Journal of Business*, 39, January, pp. 119–38.

Shiller, R. J., 1981a: Do stock prices move too much to be justified by subsequent changes in dividends? *American Economic Review*, 71(3), June, pp. 421–36.

Shiller, R. J., 1981b: The use of volatility measures in assessing market efficiency. *Journal of Finance*, 36(2), May, pp. 291–304.

Shiller, R. J., 1984: Stock prices and social dynamics. *Brookings Papers on Economic Activity*, 2, pp. 457–89.

Shiller, R. J., 1988: Fashions, fads, and bubbles in financial markets. In

Coffee et al. (eds): *Knights, Raiders and Targets*, Oxford, Oxford University Press, pp. 55–68.

Slovic, P., and S. Lichenstein, 1968: The relative importance of probabilities and pay-offs in risk-taking. *Journal of Experimental Psychology*, 78, supplement November part 2, pp. 1–18.

Summers, L. H., 1986: Do we really know that financial markets are efficient? In J. Edwards et al. (eds): *Recent Developments in Corporate Finance*, Cambridge, Cambridge University Press, pp. 13–29.

Sunder, S., 1973: Relationship between accounting changes and stock prices: Problems of measurement and some empirical evidence. *Empirical Research in Accounting: Selected Studies*, supplement to vol. 10 of *Journal of Accounting Research*, pp. 1–45.

Tinic, S. M., and R. West, 1984: Risk and return: January and the rest of the year. *Journal of Financial Economics*, 13(4), pp. 561–74.

Tobin, J., 1958: Liquidity preference as behaviour towards risk. *Review of Economic Studies*, 25, pp. 65–85.

Tversky, A., P. Slovic and D. Kahneman, 1990: The causes of preference reversal. *American Economic Review*, 80(1), March, pp. 204–17.

Vasicek, O. A., 1973: A note on using cross sectional information in Bayesian estimation of security betas. *Journal of Finance*, 28, December, p. 1233.

von Neumann, J., and O. Morgenstern, 1947: *The Theory of Games and Economic Behaviour*, 2nd edn, Princeton, Princeton University Press.

Ward, C. W., and A. Saunders, 1976: UK unit trust performance 1964–1974. *Journal of Business Finance and Accounting*, 5(4), Winter, pp. 83–100.

West, K. D., 1988: Bubbles, fads and stock market volatility tests: A partial evaluation. *Journal of Finance*, 43(3), July, pp. 639–56.

Working, H., 1934: A random difference series for use in the analysis of time series. *Journal of the American Statistical Association*, 29, March, pp. 11–24.

Zarowin, P., 1989: Does the stock market overreact to corporate earnings information? *Journal of Finance*, 44(5), December, pp. 1385–99.

Author index

Subject index